. . . .

WINNING BASKETBALL DRILLS
FROM NABC COACHES

Edited by

Jerry Krause

United States Military Academy

West Point, New York

and

James H. Conn

Central Missouri State University

Warrensburg, Missouri

. . . .

. . . .

ISBN: 1-58518-259-1
Library of Congress Catalog Card Number: 00-106281

Cover Design: Britt Johnson and Chuck Peters
Cover Photos: Brian Spurlock
Layout and Design: Deborah M. Oldenburg

Coaches Choice
P.O. Box 1828
Monterey, CA 93942
www.coacheschoiceweb.com

. . . .

DEDICATION

Jerry Krause

As NABC Research Chair for over thirty years, it has been my privilege to lead in and serve the sport I love. This book is dedicated to all the NABC coaches who are the backbone of the High School and College game and provide the positive leadership to enrich the lives of the players they are privileged to coach.

James Conn

During my thirty years of professional life of teaching/coaching and preparing young men and women to coach basketball, the NABC membership for their years of unselfishness, perseverance, self-discipline, and passion for which they have enriched the lives of the players they have served and the coaches they have uplifted. The NABC is truly the guardian and enabler of America's game.

ACKNOWLEDGMENTS

The coeditors gratefully acknowledge the support and endorsement of the National Association of Basketball Coaches (NABC) Board of Directors, especially Executive Director Jim Haney, who have been concerned with projects like this to ensure that NABC is the Guardian of the *Game*.

Appreciation also goes to the Naismith Basketball Hall of Fame, its Executive Director Joe O'Brien and Curator Doug Stark, who have been most cooperative in providing archival resources.

Finally, the most thanks go to all NABC coaches who have provided their winning drills to share with other coaches to enrich the game.

CONTENTS

· ·

·   **5**

Chapter 1—Fundamental Drills (cont.)

Chapter 1—Fundamental Drills (cont.)

Chapter 2—Offensive Drills (Drills 38-52)

Chapter 2–Offensive Drills (cont.)

Chapter 3–Defensive Drills (Drills 53-72)

Chapter 3–Defensive Drills (cont.)

Chapter 4–Combination Drills (Drills 73-82)

Chapter 4–Combination Drills (cont.)

FOREWORD

· ·

As Guardians of the Game, the NABC continues to sponsor projects to improve basketball. This project, directed by the NABC Research Chairman, is one of those projects. This collection of drills, from Hall of Famers to coaches at all NABC membership categories, is intended to help you improve your coaching and test your ideas. Best wishes for success.

Dennis Crum
1999 - 2000 NABC President
Basketball Coach, University of Louisville

INTRODUCTION

Basketball drills are only tools for a coach to use to teach the fundamental skills and tactics. Drills need to be adapted to your coaching philosophy and system of play. This drill collection is a living history of the game; drills from the coaching pioneers, as well as newer coaches; drills from high school and college coaches and also from professional level coaches.

BEFORE WE
GET STARTED...

The following three articles illustrate the importance of drill selection and use in each system of play. These specific examples are:

1. Ralph Miller, *Winter '82 Basketball Bulletin.* Note how this Hall of Fame coach adapts and simplifies drills for use in his system, as shown in his clinic on The Passing Game.

2. Bob Jones, *Winter '73 Basketball Bulletin.* This article, "Getting the Most Out Of Practice," emphasizes the need to "devise, revise, and substitute various drills to meet particular needs and interests." Coach Jones was the 1973 College Division Coach of the Year, when his team won the national championship.

3. Rob Judson, *May-June '93 Basketball Courtside.* Rob was at Bradley University and reminds us of prioritizing practice and drills during the modern era of coaching.

The Passing Game
Ralph Miller, Oregon State University

Passing is our chief weapon on offensive attacks. The first responsibility of a player is to create a situation so he can pass to a teammate for a shot. This exudes a team feeling. Seventy-five percent of our baskets last year came from assists.

Passing and catching head the list of offensive skill requirements. You can teach both with the same drills. I have found that more errors are caused by catching than passing.

Two learning laws that we apply to our practices and drills are:

1. Any physical act has to be learned the hard way—learn by doing.

2. Repetition—over and over again.

Skills are only part of the whole. You have to apply them to competition. A coach is responsible to condition skill reaction in competition. The reaction is actually more important than the skill. You as a coach are a teacher and you should know the subject material and know how to best teach that material.

While I was coaching in high school, I began to ask myself several questions. Why use pressure defenses only part of the time? (At that time, teams dropped back after missed baskets.) Why not pressure all the time on defense? Why not pressure with offense as well as defense? We came up with the idea of instant conversion either way as the ball changes hands. We wanted all of our offensive patterns to start with the break. I didn't create anything new. I just looked into the past and used ideas. I took these ideas with me to college in 1951 and haven't changed since.

Our system is based on the pass and cut. In my opinion, the pass and cut are the two most difficult things to defense in basketball. There are three ways to create offensive openings: (1) One-on-one dribbling. (2) screens. (3) Pass and cut. Even though we feel pass and cut is the most important, we want to put all three together.

In our system the player must be able to shoot, pass or drive the moment the ball touches his hand. We have our players use the "jump stop." The key result is the time it takes to get the shot off. A player should be able to shoot in one second as soon as it hits his hands. The secret of successful shooting is to get ready as the ball is being passed to you. Once the man has the ball we authorize only two fakes—fake the shot and fake the pass.

We want to teach three areas: (1) Skills. (2) Competitive reactions. (3) Related knowledge (When? Where? How?). We feel the following six drills do these three things.

Drill #1: Two-Lane Shooting Drill (Figure A)

•   Use two balls.

•   45-degree angle running at full speed.

•   Work from the left side also.

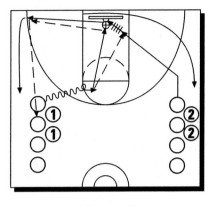

Figure A

- Must make 30 layups or so in a row before team moves on to another drill.

Drill #2: Split the Post (Figure B)

- (1) passes the ball to (2) and follows the ball.

- (2) dribbles the ball to (1) position and then passes the ball back to the man who originally passed the ball to (2) in the (2) position.

- (1) passes to (5) in the free-throw circle and (1) and (2) then split off the post.

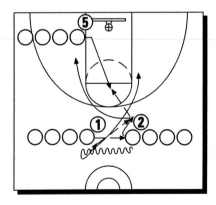

Figure B

When the two men out front exchange lines (positions), they use jump stops and reverse pivots to face each other again. In this drill we practice three types of shots: layups, short hooks, short 17-foot jump shots. Post men slide to basketball side, receive pass and work on their shots.

Drill #3: Breaking Drill (Figure C)

- The ball never touches the floor and players go at full speed.

- Down and back is one trip. Go until group has 30 error-free trips.

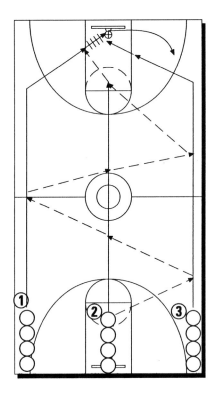

Figure C

Drill #4: Wide Three-Man Weave (Figure D)

Down and back. Run it wide. Again, require players to make a certain number in a row before you move on to another drill. Two things are accomplished by requiring players to make a certain number in a row—it builds the team concept and lets the team know who is the boss.

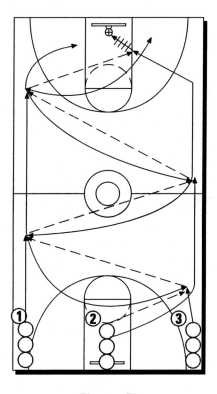

Figure D

Drill #5: Three-on-Three Full Court (Figure E).

- The fifth and sixth drills are the bread and butter drills.

- Players cannot pass the ball over the mid-court line; they must dribble the ball.

- Players must switch on all good screens.

- If the offense gets the rebound, same players remain on defense.

- If the offense misses the shot, the defense tries to fast break while the "new" defensive players pick up the man who was guarding them.

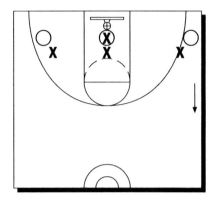

Figure E

Drill #6: Four-on-Four Full Court (Figure F)

- Always start at half-court and go half-court to full-court.

- Go up and down the court three or four times, then change all eight players.

- These six drills teach the skills that are necessary to play the game.

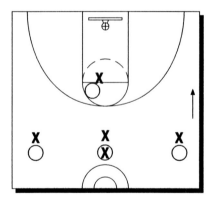

Figure F

Getting the Most Out of Practice
Bob Jones, Kentucky Wesleyan College
1973 NABC College Division Coach of the Year

We feel that our practice schedule is as important as any other aspect of our basketball program. We believe games are won in practice. In order to get maximum benefit from our practices, while keeping negative effects to a minimum, we usually try to limit practice to one hour and 45 minutes per day. As a former player, I know from personal experience what it means to keep practice time down to the two-hour mark. You develop a more positive attitude toward practice when you know it will not exceed two hours.

The shorter practice session is practical; however, only under certain conditions. First, the players must be sufficiently motivated. I believe the most important part of our coaching lies in motivation and establishing mutual respect. If your players believe in you and your philosophy, the shorter practice session is workable.

Second, 100 percent concentration is required of all involved—coaches, players, managers. Practice is a business, and no talking or horseplay is permitted on the practice floor. Finally, daily organization by the coaching staff is essential. The entire coaching staff takes part in a daily planning session in which the practice schedule is formulated. As always in such situations, the final decision as to how much time is to be spent on fundamentals or on a specific weakness will lie with the head coach. This daily schedule is then posted outside our dressing room prior to every practice session. In this way, each player knows what we will be doing and what amount of time will be spent on each segment of practice. This is necessary because one important aspect of our practice philosophy is to keep our players from pacing themselves.

In a typical practice, we run a series of drills called "quick drills," with which we attempt to work on fundamentals, conditioning, and shooting. We organize these drills in special order to allow for rest. An example of these "quick drills" follows:

1. Four-corner layups (3 min.). This is a drill in which A dribbles in and shoots a layup, gets his own rebound and passes to B, and goes to the back of line B. B then passes to C and goes to the back of line C. C passes to D and goes to the back of line D. D passes to A and goes to the back of line A. This starts the whole process again (Figure G).

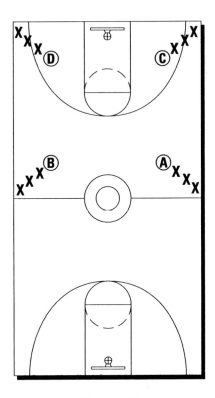

Figure G

2. Two-man passing (2 min.). Focus on spacing, passing and catching.

3. Touch and go (2 min.)—slow men, 40 sec.; medium men, 37 sec.; fast men, 35 sec.

4. Foul shooting (3 min.).

5. Ball tag (3 min.). We play a game of tag with the basketball. One person will be "it" and will try to catch everyone else, rotating right hand and left hand.

6. Five-man weave (3 min.). This is a figure eight drill using five men.

7. Defensive slide (90 sec.). This is a continuous defensive movement drill.

8. Pressure shooting (3 min.). We emphasize working under pressure a great deal. In this drill, we use pressure feeding on our shooting. Two players feed one, forcing him to shoot the shot quickly without a dribble. The shooter

must move and not remain in one spot. We stress technique and follow-through in shooting.

9.   Pickups (3 min.). This is an old baseball drill in which one player rolls the ball and another slides in front and throws it back. This continues for three minutes, with each player alternating 25 pickups each.

10.   Foul shooting (3 min.).

11.   Touch and go (3 min.)—slow men, 42 sec.; medium men, 38 sec.; fast men, 36 sec.

12.   Three-man tip (3 min.). You begin this drill with two men, one on one side of the basket and one on the other. Start the ball on the side with two men. Each man tips the ball over the basket and then slides across to the other side, continuing this for 12 tips and making it on the 13th.

13.   One line tip (4 min.). This drill is used to work on timing in the jump.

Because the mental aspect is just as important as the physical in basketball, we employ several methods to prevent monotony and/or boredom. *It is the coach's job to devise, revise and substitute various drills to meet particular needs and interests.* We also change practice time occasionally during the season, even mix in a night practice once in a while. We also give the players an occasional day off and we expect it to be just that. We do not have them shoot or run a drill that day. We don't even want them around a gym on their days off.

We followed this practice philosophy last year and feel it had a great deal to do with our winning the 1973 College Division Championship.

Practice Priorities Help Save Precious Time
Rob Judson, Bradley University

Organization of your team's practice, both before your first game and during the season, has become critical to success on the court.

NCAA legislation has limited practice time in two ways:

- Moving the start of practice back to November 1, while allowing the first game the weekend after Thanksgiving.

- Daily and weekly time limitations during the season.

Since a coaching staff's time is limited, the importance of a practice plan based on your team's priorities becomes crucial.

Head coaches and their staffs cannot afford to waste precious practice time. In order to be most efficient each day of practice, staffs must evaluate which areas need to be emphasized. This will lead to individual play development and the resultant team improvement on the court. A program's offensive and defensive system will be effective when the parts are emphasized at practice. This is a must, as well as stressing individual player improvement through fundamental skill work.

To organize this evaluation process, define your team's needs in two areas: fundamental priorities and team priorities. The fundamental priority area is made up of ballhandling, offensive fundamentals and defensive fundamentals. The team priority area is made up of offensive and defensive team priorities. Each aspect of the game is prioritized in the charts below.

Fundamental Priorities

Ballhandling
Ballhandling drills
Dribbling
Passing, pass-fakes

Offense
Footwork

Offense (cont.)
Free throws
Offensive moves on the dribble
Offensive rebounding
Post moves
Reading the defense, screens
Shooting form
Shot selection
Stationary offensive moves
Three-point shooting

Defense

Ball screens
Boxing out
Taking the charge
Footwork
Off-ball defense
On-ball defense
Post defense
Shooter defense—closeout
Stance

Team Priorities

Defense

Man-to-man press—run and jump
Team defense—help rotation
Three-point defense
Transition
Zone defenses
Zone press
Zone traps

Offense

Delay
Entries
Fast break—primary
Free throw fast break

Offense (cont.)

Man-to-man offense
Out-of-bounds plays
Press breaker
Secondary break
Spread offense
Three-point philosophy
Zone offense
Situations

Before November 1, a coaching staff should evaluate its team's strengths and weaknesses in each area, then place the team's greatest weakness at the top of that area's priorities. You should continue to determine the team's most urgent concern through each priority area. When you have finished, you will have determined your team's priorities for practice before the first game. A team's offensive fundamental area may look like this:

1. Footwork

2. Shot form

3. Shot selection

4. Three-point shooting

5. Offensive rebounding

6. Post moves

7. Free throws

8. Stationary offensive moves

9. Reading the defense

10. Offensive moves on the dribble

These priorities would indicate a team's needs in developing shooting, along with an emphasis on offensive rebounding and post play. As a coach develops his practice plan, time is given to the highest priority whenever there is a conflict.

Since it is impossible to cover every area during each practice, alternating the offensive and defensive fundamentals with the offensive and defensive team concepts is helpful (e.g., offensive fundamentals combined with defensive team play one day, and defensive fundamentals with offensive team play the next day.)

In the two to three weeks prior to the first game, you will drill each fundamental area. The staff also will implement its various team offensive and defensive concepts. By prioritizing these concepts and areas, coaches ensure a logical practice scheme before the first game.

Once games begin, evaluation of your team's priorities becomes an ongoing process. Priorities in each area will change throughout the season, and they should. Your team will improve in areas as you work on them in practice each day.

Practicing priorities also allows a coach to emphasize areas of slippage after games. A poor rebounding performance results in offensive rebounding, boxing out and closeouts moving up in the fundamental priority area for the next practice. Poor execution of primary fast-break situations gives that a higher emphasis at practice, and so on.

The evaluation of your team's priorities will prove especially helpful when you hit the thick of your schedule. Time constraints and limited days of preparation make it crucial to organize your priorities for practice before each opponent. Different teams and their systems force you to adjust practice priorities. A pressing, trapping team would make you emphasize ballhandling fundamentals, along with your out-of-bounds plays and press breakers.

Coaches may feel that they already adjust their priorities to these various factors. Every program does in some manner. It is the extent to which a logical, organized plan for practice priorities is used that will determine success during a season. Practicing your team's priorities gives you the opportunity to win games where your team's success or failure all begins or ends—on the practice floor.

PLAY DESCRIPTION KEY

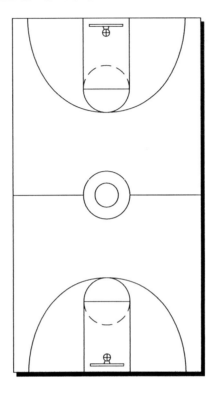

○ = **Offense**

X = **Defense**

⊙ = **Player with the Ball**

– – → = **Direct Pass**

———⊣ = **Screen**

〜〜〜→ = **Dribble**

———▻ = **Cut of Player with or without the Ball**

╫╫╫╫╫▻ = **Shot**

CHAPTER 1

FUNDAMENTAL DRILLS

Drill #1: 100% Game

Purpose:

To teach accuracy and versatility in the use of fundamentals.

Description:

- The players work in squads of five. Each squad uses its own basket, and all squads compete for the highest team scores. Each player competes for his squad on a scale of 100 points for a perfect individual score.

- As shown in Figure 1-A, 10 positions for each squad are outlined on the floor, where 10 specified fundamentals will be executed by each man on the squad. Thus, each player will get tries at different shots or plays from each of the various positions. Each successful try counts 10 points toward his individual score and 10 points toward his team's total score. A violation or a penalty incurred by one of the competing men will take 10 points off his individual score.

- The coach of the drill should pass the ball to the player who, during his various attempts, will swing into positions that simulate every possible game condition. After each try, the player should throw the ball back to the coach before beginning his new try. Each player, when in position to score, must shoot by the time he hears the count of three. A violation of technical play during a try invalidates that try, even though it has been successful.

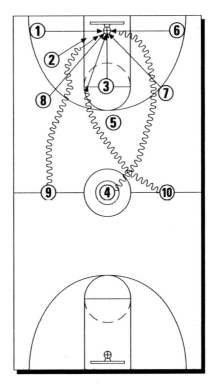

Figure 1-A

The O's used on the diagram indicate the specified areas on the floor from which the players will work, and the numbers indicate the order in which the play will be made. A tentative shooting program is outlined here, but may be changed as conditions warrant.

1. Player standing in corner of court within 3—5 feet of the end and sidelines receives the ball and takes a shot there.

2. Player standing in court on the left side, between corner and free throw line, uses a backboard shot.

3. Player standing back of free throw line makes a free throw try for goal.

4. Player standing back of the center of the court receives a bounce pass from the coach of the drill and dribbles without opposition down the court to the

side of the basket. As the player nears the basket, he uses the one-hand layup shot against the backboard in a try for goal.

5.   Player stands near the free throw line, ready to break up an opponent's dribble. He can advance or retreat to keep the dribbler from scoring. If the guard prevents the dribbler from scoring, 10 points are added to the guard's score. Merely dribbling past the guard does not make his try a failure. The dribbler must also cage the ball before the guard has lost his chance to increase his score.

6.   Player, standing in position in opposite corner from which try, Play 1 was made, attempts a corner shot.

7.   Player repeats his Play 2 on the opposite side at the same relative angle, but further out in the court.

8.   Player, standing about 20 feet from the basket and at an angle of 45 degrees with the surface of the backboard. He does not aim to play the backboard, but intends to make a three-point field goal shot.

9.   Player takes the ball, on the bounce, from the coach back of the center circle. He will attempt a successful dribble past a guard who has been stationed near the goal-zone line.

10. The player again receives the ball on a bounce pass, back of center. The guard on the free throw line is instructed not to advance too far to meet the dribbler. The dribbler advances down the center of the court. When he gets within shooting range, yet still far enough in front of the basket so that the guard on the free throw line cannot block the ball, the dribbler rises on one foot and raises the ball high in the air for a floater. He then cuts around the guard for rebound work. The guard will resist him in this effort. Either the direct hit or the goal from the follow shot will count as a perfect score on this try.

These competitive drills should always be conducted as team or squad events and not as individual contests. If so handled, the stronger players will coach the weaker in shooting, so as to improve their own team percentages. The commanding desire is to win, and this is the first incentive toward cooperation or teamwork (see Figure 1-A).

Coach:

Dr. Forrest "Phog" Allen, a longtime coach at the University of Kansas, was elected to the Basketball Hall of Fame in 1959. He was the first basketball coach in the country, at Baker University (KS).

NOTE: This drill, exactly as written, was taken from his book *"Better Basketball,"* which was one of the first basketball coaching books.

Drill #2: Offensive Footwork and Maneuvering

Purpose:

To teach players to reverse pivot and execute a front and rear turn.

Description:

- The reverse pivot is executed from the one-count quick stop position. The front foot is the pivot foot. (The stride stop must be one-count in order to pivot on the front foot; in the two-count stop only the rear foot can be used legally.) The rear foot is swung to a position parallel or in advance of the pivot foot, and is done in such a manner as to place the body between the defensive man and the ball. The player is now facing the opposite direction from which he started. He has reversed himself by the pivoting—thus the name "reverse pivot." (See Figure 2-A.)

- The front players in each line dribble 15–20 feet, make a one-count quick stop or stride stop, and execute a good reverse pivot. Upon completing the pivot, they pivot back to their original stop position, then continue to dribble and stop down the floor and back. First players pass to the next player in their line and go to the end of the line. (See Figure 2-B.)

Coaching Cues:

The body remains low, and as the pivot is completed, the weight is transferred from the original front foot to the new front foot.

Coach:

Fred "Tex" Winter was an assistant basketball coach with the Chicago Bulls. Tex is now coaching with Phil Jackson for the Los Angeles Lakers. He is credited with inventing the "triangle post" offense, which the Bulls used to win four consecutive NBA Championships. Tex was selected as the NABC Golden Anniversary Coach in 1999.

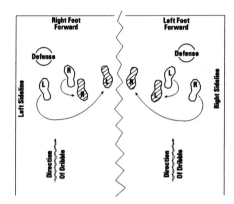

Figure 2-A
Reverse Pivot Drill

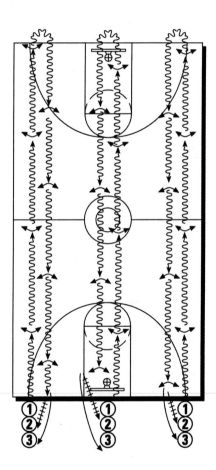

Figure 2-B

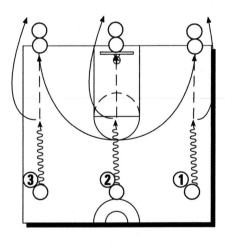

Figure 2-B
Circuit Completion

Drill #3: All-Purpose

Purpose:

To teach dribbling, quick stopping, faking a pass, pivoting on both feet, screening, defending and shooting.

Description:

- Each group is given a ball. Two players in each group are stationed as guards in tandem across the court in front of their groups. The guards should divide the distance across the court into equal thirds, so that the distance from the first guard to the player with the ball is equal to the distance between the guards, and this distance in turn is equal to the distance between the second guard and the other side of the court.

- On the command of "go," all start dribbling toward their first guard. As they approach that defender, they all cut to their left. The guard moves over to prevent the dribbler from going around. At first the guard should play a passive game. As the players become adept at the drill and at the various techniques of the drill, then more competition and opposition may be offered. The dribbler stops and fakes a pass forward. He then pivots. The next man in the line is directed to trail about 10–15 feet directly back of the dribbler at all times. As the dribbler pivots, the trailer darts by him and receives the ball. The trailer now becomes the dribbler and approaches the second defender. The first defender has finished his job, so goes to the back of the line of his group. The first dribbler now becomes the trailer. As the second defender is approached, all dribblers cut to the right (the dribbler's right). The defender moves over to prevent the dribbler from going around. The dribbler stops, fakes and pivots back. The trailer now comes through for the ball. As the ball is handed to him, the pivoter, after passing the ball, continues with the dribbler to keep between him and the defender. He thus acts as a screen, and the trailer may continue in toward the side goal and shoot.

- At the finish of the shot, whoever recovers the ball throws a catcher's baseball pass back to the player across the court in the front of the line. The second defender now goes to the end of the line, and the two players who were handling the ball (offensive players) become the two guards for the next drill. (See Figure 3-A.)

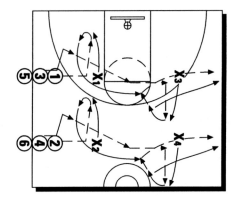

Figure 3-A
All-Purpose Drill

Coaching Cues:

1.   All groups should work simultaneously.

2.   Designate players to give the commands each time.

3.   Start slowly, and gradually work toward speed and snappiness.

Coach:

John Bunn coached at Springfield College, Stanford University, and Colorado State College. Coach Bunn is a member of the Basketball Hall of Fame and was the basketball rules editor for over 15 years.

Drill #4: Zigzag

Purpose:

To teach the proper movement out of the pressure defensive stance.

Description:

• Player 1 is a dribbler and player X1 is a defender. The court is divided invisibly down the middle and player 1 is not allowed to dribble across the invisible line.

- Player 1 dribbles the length of the court in a zigzag pattern.

- Player X1, in his defensive stance, slides with the dribbler to the opposite end of the floor. (See Figure 4-A.)

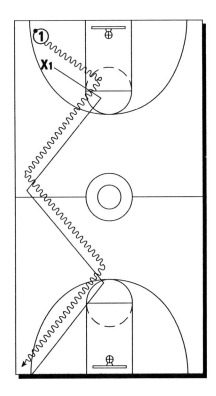

Figure 4-A
Offensive-Defensive Zigzag

Coaching Cues:

1. The defensive player must always stand close enough to the offensive player so that he could put his palm on the offensive player's chest.

2. The defensive player must keep his head directly between the ball and the basket.

3. Players must apply constant pressure to the ball with their hands. The defensive player, playing palms up, pressures the ball with the hand nearest

the direction the offensive player is moving. For example, if the offensive player moves to the right, the defensive player uses his right hand to flick the ball.

4. Players should not cross their feet when moving or changing direction.

5. If the offensive player turns his back on a reverse, the defensive player must retreat one step to avoid getting caught by the offensive step drop.

Coach:

Bob Knight is the head basketball coach at Indiana University. Knight is the winningest basketball coach in Indiana history. He was elected to the Basketball Hall of Fame in 1991 and also led the 1984 USA Olympic team to the Gold Medal. His Indiana teams have won three national championships.

Drill #5: Full-Court Ballhandling/Defense

Purpose:

To teach the principles and techniques of moving with the ball and defending full court.

Description:

Players work in pairs. The coach throws ball out to different spots. 1 recovers ball and drives to basket with X1 in pursuit (chaser). 1 attacks the basket with defense in hot pursuit. 1 makes basket and sprints out of bounds mid-corner area. X1 (chaser) recovers the ball and passes to 1, holding position out of bounds until pass is received. 1 speed dribbles up sideline upon a receipt of ball. X1 pursues the dribble and attempts to cut dribbler off as soon as possible and continues to play defense on 1. 1 can attempt to beat defensive player on dribble drive or pass ball to Coach 2, and speed out to basket. X1 defenses 1 on the dribble or on the pass and cut. X1 attempts to score and then goes to the end of the line. X1 recovers ball and passes to Coach X, and goes to offensive position at end of the line.

Drill continues. Keep two balls going on this drill once player becomes familiar with it (Figure 5-A).

Coaching Cues:

1. Use speed dribble on straight line to the basket.

2. Defender attempts to get between offense ball handler and basket.

3. Sprint and turn the dribbler when on defense.

4. Block out.

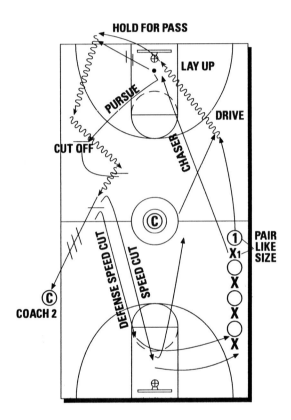

Figure 5-A

Coach:

Fred "Tex" Winter was an assistant coach with the Chicago Bulls for 12 years, during which they won six NBA Championships. This last year the NABC honored Tex for completing his 50th season coaching basketball at the Division I collegiate or professional level. Tex coached at Kansas State, Marquette, University of Washington, Northwestern, California State University–Long Beach, Louisiana State University, and for the San Diego Rockets, Houston Rockets, and Chicago Bulls. He is now with the Los Angeles Lakers.

Drill #6: Multiple Balls

Purpose:

To teach accurate passing and catching skills under fatigue conditions.

Description:

One to five balls may be used. The players are lined up as shown in Figure 6-A. In the illustration three balls are being used. The middle player (5) starts the drill by passing to 6 or 7. Passes are made from the front line in the continuity shown 1, 2, 3 and 4. The tempo is speeded up until 5 cannot maintain the passing pressure and makes a mistake. All passes may be used and the frontline players must be alert in timing their passes, as well as catching the ball from one of the back-line teammates. Positions are rotated so that every player works in the various positions.

Coaching Cues:

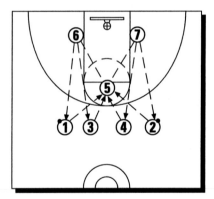

Figure 6-A

Hands up, knees bent, ready to pass and catch.

Coach:

Clair Bee was elected to the Basketball Hall of Fame in 1967 as a contributor. He was renowned as a coaching genius at Long Island University.

Note: This drill, which coaches regularly use today, originated in the early years of basketball.

Drill #7: Chin-It Rebounding

Purpose:

To teach players a ball protection technique that is effective in rebounding or whenever pressured by defenders.

Description:

Chin-it technique is done by being in a quick stance (feet shoulders' width apart, weight on whole foot, all joints flexed) with both hands on the ball and elbows out (be an eagle). The ball is placed firmly under the chin with fingers up and elbows out. Chin-it can be taught by:

- Having all players assume a chin-it position (with or without a ball) whenever the coach blows the whistle—teaches instant chin-it reaction and gets players' immediate attention. Each player can use pivots and turns after assuming the chin-it position to face the coach directly. (See Figure 7-A.)

- Using chin-it technique when offensive rebounding. For example, in Figure 7-B, players use a two-hand, underhand toss near top of backboard to create a rebound. O1 and O2 angle jump to capture the ball with two hands, chin the ball and go up to score with a power move. Feet are at right angles to the baseline; rebound with two hands and two feet. After scoring, pass to next player in line and go to back of opposite line.

- In Figure 7-C, the defensive rebound is created with a toss off backboard, then two hand, two feet rebound, chin-it, and making an outlet pass (X1 to X5). X5 passes to X2, then to X6 and back to X2. Note that all players who are receiving a pass make a move to get open V-cut. The drill is then repeated on the other side.

Critical Cues:

Chin-it—fingers up (keeps player from dangling the ball and maintains chin-it position) and elbows out.

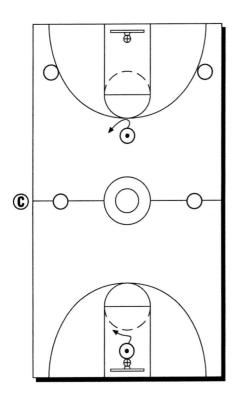

Figure 7-A
Whistle Chin-It

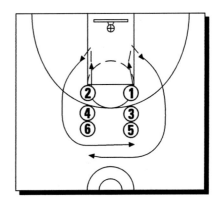

Figure 7-B
Offensive Rebound
(chin and score)

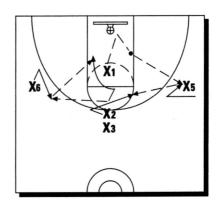

Figure 7-C
Defensive Rebound
(chin and outlet)

Coach:

Jerry Krause has coached at all levels of basketball and has been NABC Research Chair for 30 years. Jim Conn is a former assistant coach who has coached at the high school and college levels.

Drill #8: 1 versus 2 Pivoting

Purpose:

To teach players to be strong with the ball while under duress from defensive pressure.

Description:

See Figure 8-A. P, the passer, pivots with the ball and faces the defense until the coach blows the whistle. X1 and X2 slap, grab, foul and try to knock the passer off balance. On the whistle, P delivers a pass to B1 or B2. B1 or B2 must make a scoring move at X3.

X1, X2 and X3 can be managers or other players.

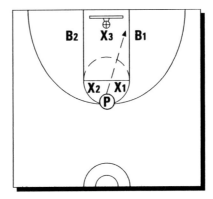

Figure 8-A

Coaching Cues:

Ball handler/passer

1. Triple threat with the ball tight to the body.

2. Head up.

3. Tight pivoting.

4. When moving the ball from one side of your body to the other, rip it through tight to the body.

5.   Fake a pass to make a pass.

Bigs (Post Players)

1.   Start with butts to baseline.

2.   Catch and square shoulders to baseline.

3.   Score with your outside hand and go up and through the defense.

4.   Use your inside leg as a kickstand to acquire balance before finishing.

5.   Finish above the rim on your scoring move.

Coach:

Herb Sendek is the head basketball coach at North Carolina State University, where John Grace is an assistant basketball coach. Their teams are known for aggressive defense.

Drill #9: Hamburger

Purpose:

To teach players to score under physical pressure, offensive rebounding, aggressiveness.

Description:

• Three to six players are placed in three lines at the basket. Start the drill by putting the ball on the floor. 1 picks ball up and scores. If he misses, any of the other 1's can rebound and score. After the 1's score, they go to the end of the line and 2 then repeats. After 1, 2, 3 score, the ball then goes to the middle line and then to the left side. (See Figure 9-A.)

• For the next round we move back and take the 15-foot jump shot, but now the ball is passed to the shooter. The next shot is the three-point shot (see Figure 9-B).

• If a rebound goes long, whoever hustles to capture it passes to teammates, who spread out and go in for a layup (or the man who gets the long rebound can go 1-on-2).

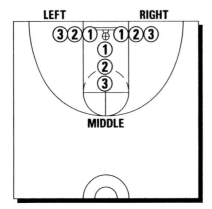

Figure 9-A
Baseline Shots

Figure 9-B
15 ft. shot/3 pt. FG
45-degree angle shot

Coaching Cues:

1. Score under pressure with defender contact.

2. Always assume shot will be missed, so be ready to rebound (hands up, knees bent).

Coach:

Jim Smith has coached at St. John's University in Collegeville, Minnesota, since 1964 and has accumulated over 536 wins.

Drill #10: Manipulation (Four-Corner)

Purpose:

To teach players to move the feet, use the eyes, arms, hands and wrists to pass and receive ball correctly.

Description:

Figure 10-A. Coach (C) starts in the middle and moves left, with good defensive shuffle. He hits X1. X1 hits C back, and C hits X1 right back as he makes semicircle to back of X2's line. This is repeated until all X1's are X2's, X2's are X3's, X3's are X4's and X4's are X1's. Passes are not shown for the sake of clarity, but we use a two-handed chest pass exclusively in this drill.

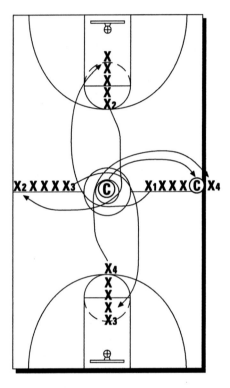

Figure 10-A

Coaching Cues:

1.   Pass quickly, accurately and with good follow-through.

2.   Catch passes with vision and both hands.

Coach:

Dave Strack is the former basketball coach at the University of Michigan. He coached the great Cazzie Russell.

Drill #11: Let Your Feet Do the Walking

Purpose:

To teach players basic stance and steps/footwork for basketball.

Description:

Pete Newell, coach of the U.S. Olympic Team Gold Medal winner and a leading authority on basketball in the U.S., has been conducting footwork camps to assist professional basketball players! In essence, the pros have been returning to this basic school because their own coaches either did not have the time or commitment to go over this fundamental skill. You quickly realize the importance of front pivots, reverse pivots and drop steps when you see professionals working at them.

Your team can develop sound footwork and body balance within a relatively short period of time if you dedicate your squad to some simple drills on a daily basis.

The following information was taken from John Wooden, Pete Newell and Ed Goorjian; these men espoused the fundamentals—not only on the court, but off the court as well.

Footwork

- Warm-up Run—baseline to baseline, stop; baseline to baseline (i.e., first person in each line must wait until last person of every line finishes). (See Figure 11-A.)

- Angle Cuts—baseline to baseline, stop; baseline to baseline. (See Figure 11-B).

- Jump Stops—free throw, half-court, free throw, baseline (same procedure on the way back). (See Figure 11-C.)

- Front Pivots—free throw, half-court, free throw, baseline (same procedure on the way back). (See Figure 11-D.)

- Reverse Pivots—free throw, half-court, free throw, baseline (same procedure on the way back). (See Figure 11-E.)

- Stride Pivots—free throw, half-court, free throw, baseline (same procedure on the way back). (See Figures 11-F, 11-G.)

Figure 11-A, Warm-up Run

Run to opposite baseline, moving arms in windmill fashion. Stop once you get to baseline and re-form line. Can use change-of-pace runs. Once first person crosses free throw line, the next person follows. Divide lines up according to numbers (i.e., you might have six lines).

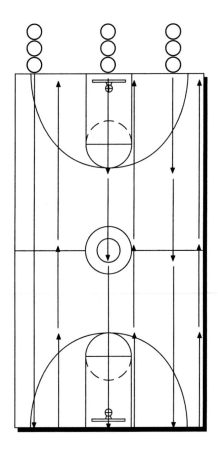

Figure 11-A   **Figure 11-B**

Chapter 1—Fundamental Drills

Figure 11-B, Angle Cuts

Hands chest level, diagonal cuts with emphasis on cutting sharply on the outside foot, stop at the opposite baseline. Same procedure on the way back, but wait until line forms completely (see example) before group starts back to original baseline.

Figure 11-C, Two-Foot Jump Stop (down and back)

Body Balance—feet = shoulders' width; legs-knees flexed; butt down; back straight; head up; hands in triple threat position (i.e., like you are holding an imaginary ball in "ready position" —shooting position).

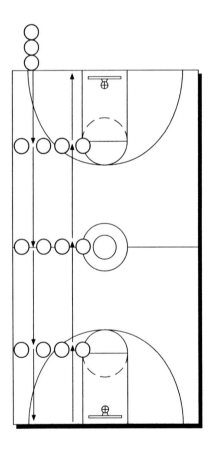

Figure 11-C

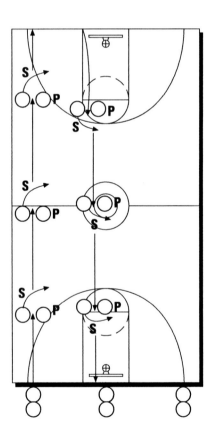

Figure 11-D

Run, under control, to the free throw line and jump stop. Both feet hit the floor at the same time. Important to emphasize that you do not hop to a stop, but rather **skim** to a stop. Body weight transferred to butt area, **head must be up** or you will be off balance. Check hand position (imaginary ball); always ready to shoot; a definite building block for later lectures.

Figure 11-D, Front Pivots

Run to free throw line, jump stop. Right foot swings around (now facing line of people) while left is planted—pivot foot.

Stay low and balanced. Keep feet at least shoulders width apart. Hold hands in triple-threat position. Keep head up.

Part 2—will front pivot again (360 degrees—same direction; Part 1 —180 degrees). Emphasize fundamentals. MOST IMPORTANT: GO SLOW. NOT A RACE. Free throw, half-court, free throw, baseline: stop, wait until last person in **all** lines is finished before you start back.

Figure 11-E, Reverse Pivots

Run to free throw line, jump stop, reverse pivot (swing foot **drops back** to baseline from where you started). All fundamentals remain the same. Stay low and wide for body balance. Hand position, in triple threat.

Sequence is the same: free throw—reverse pivot (180 degrees— reverse pivot again 360 degrees). Run to half-court line. Same procedure and so forth. Be patient and go slow (i.e., if you get them doing this several times a day, you will see big gains).

Figures 11-F and 11-G, Stride Pivots

Most difficult, most important for shooting off the run. Instead of jump stopping, player runs under control and stops on the run. Back foot is the pivot foot; it stops or plants first (i.e., tell them on the way down you want the left foot to be the pivot foot and the right foot to be the lead foot).

Front pivot (180 degrees—Part 1—360 degrees—Part 2—full circle). Stay low and balanced. As an instructor, you can have them switch their pivot foot on way back and/or reverse pivot. Be careful, as this footwork is difficult, but vital to shoot off the run.

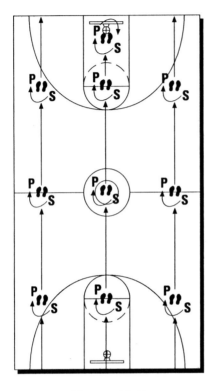

Figure 11-E

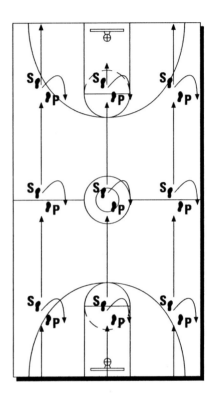

Figure 11-F

Drill #11-1: Catch and Turn (Figure 11-G)

Emphasis: Catch and turn (stay low, maintain balance, eyes up, ball in triple-threat position).

Drill #11-2: Catch, Turn and Shoot (Figure 11-H)

"Be strong with the ball." Stay low all the way through the pivot.

Emphasis: Aggressive pivot, into triple-threat position, follow through, eyes up.

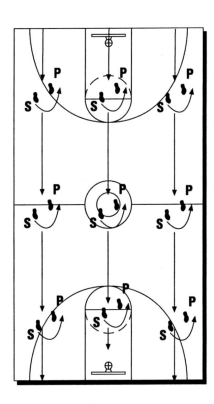

Figure 11-G

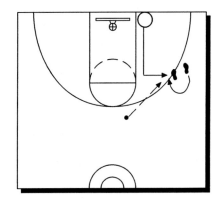

Figure 11-H

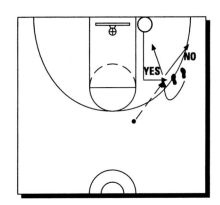

Figure 11-I

Drill #11-3: Catch, Turn and Cross Over (Figure 11-I)

The angle of the drive must be to the basket. We want to "open the defender." Always attack top foot of the defender. We want him to reverse pivot; defender must honor fake or go on him.

Emphasis: Head and shoulders fake. The fake must be done quickly with eyes up.

Drill #11-4: Turn and Go (Figure 11-J)

"Nothing else matters if you don't stay low." Head and shoulders fake, but the ball stays put.

Emphasis: Turn, read and go.

Drill #11-5: Drop Step (Figure 11-K)

When you are being overplayed, you must use the drop step to the basket (e.g., Larry Bird, the best). Feet and shoulders must point to the rim. Stay low—"sit down." Long, low dribble with the right hand.

Emphasis: Stay low; long, explosive first step—drop step.

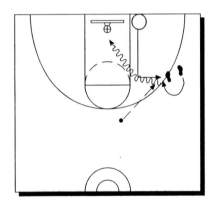

Figure 11-J

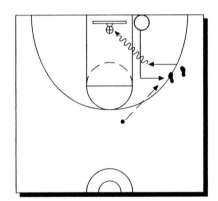

Figure 11-K

Drill #11-6: Drop Step, Square-up Jumper (Figure 11-L)

Stay low when you pull back from drop step for jump shot.

Emphasis: Low with shoulders square to rim and eyes up.

Drill #11-7: Drop Step, Fake Jump Shot and Go (Figure 11-M)

Read defense, head and shoulders fake, explode to basket.

Emphasis: Stay low, eyes up, long and low dribble, first step— quick.

Figure 11-L

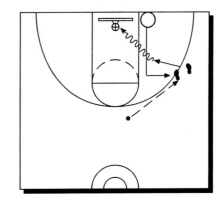

Figure 11-M

Drill #11-8: Drop Step, Square up, Drive Baseline for Jumper (Figure 11-N)

Read defense, stay low, first step is most important. Drop step always the same for every move (i.e., long, low, feet and shoulders point to the rim). Do not raise up.

Emphasis: Be quick and decisive. Eyes up.

Drill #11-9: Drop Step, Square-up and Shot Fake, Drive Baseline, Shot Fake and Shoot (Figure 11-O)

Shot Fake—head, shoulders and ball move as one. The ball should not be brought above head. Angle—drive to the basket.

Emphasis: Stay low. Don't come up with fake.

Drill #11-10: Drop Step, Square up, Drive Middle, Step-Back Move, Shoot (Figure 11-P)

Step-back move. Drive defender to the basket with one dribble, pull back and shoot. Why? Create a gap between defender and you, a S-U-P-E-R move.

Emphasis: You actually step over instead of straight back.

Drill #11-11: Drop Step, Square up, Drive Baseline, Step Back and Shoot (Figure 11-Q)

Create distance between you and the defender. Balance—do not shoot a fade-away.

Emphasis: Be smooth, use your legs.

Figure 11-N

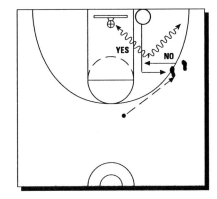

Figure 11-O

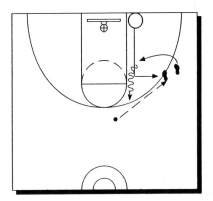

Figure 11-P

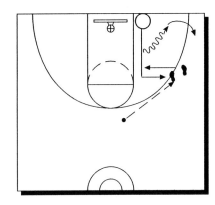

Figure 11-Q

Drill #11-12: One-on-One (Figure 11-R)

Work on your turn-in moves and/or drop-step moves. Coach Newell works on the transfer once offense works against defense. There must be a carryover of information.

Drill #11-13: Two-on-Two Stack (Figure 11-S)

Points of teaching—both players come up high to open basket up; spacing; backdoor play; must read the situation.

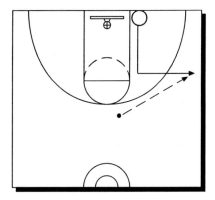

Figure 11-R   Figure 11-S

Drill #11-14: Setting a Screen (Figure 11-T)

Picker—should not be too eager to get to the ball. In other words, once you set the screen, maintain contact with defender. Set the screen, roll and seal the defender, then move him out for spacing reasons (just like you were blocking out). Don't be too eager to come to the ball and/or release contact. Receiver—better late than early; look for screener, as he will be open, shoulder-to-shoulder rub.

Emphasis: Holding contact. Spacing. Creating distance (block-out technique).

Drill #11-15: Bank Shot Drill (Figure 11-U)

Know area from where to shoot bank shot; always shoot a bank from that area— never a question in your mind. Beauty of a bank: you can be in motion and still have a good chance of making shot; softens touch and you can get it over taller players. Aim at the top of rectangle—good target.

Figure 11-T

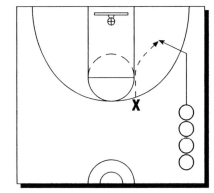

Figure 11-U

Coaching Cues:

1.   Hands must be up in **all** phases of drills (see Figures 11-A through 11-U).

2.   Triple-threat position in **all** pivot drills—ready to shoot.

3.   Body balance and footwork most important.

4.   Very important to keep lines organized; all drills done in sequence.

5.   Triple Threat—most important position you can assume on offense. "Ball-You-Man" principle.

6.   Turn into shot. Why? Closer to the basket and all your momentum going to the basket.

7.   Do some footwork drills every day. Focus on balance and execution.

Coach:

Mike Dunlap was formerly an assistant coach at the University of Southern California when this article was written.

Drill #12: Full-Court V-Cut

Purpose:

To teach players the capability of effectively changing directions and moving without the basketball.

Description:

The drill begins with the player underneath the basket throwing the ball off the glass and outletting to the first player in line at the foul line extended. When the ball is in the air or going off the glass, the player one line ahead makes a V-cut, and then by the time he steps to the ball, the player in the next line should be making a V-cut. Players should follow their passes and advance to the next line. The final pass should have the

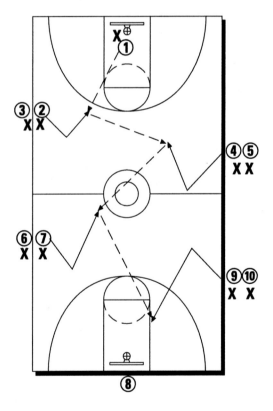

Figure 12-A
Full-Court V-cuts

cutter initially stepping to the ball, then making a backdoor cut, receiving the ball for a layup. (See Figure 12-A.)

Coaching Cues:

Use passing and movement fundamental cues. V-cut at the right time with a slow-fast change-of-direction move.

Coach:

Art Perry is the head basketball coach at American University. He has coached over 25 NBA players and is considered one of the nation's top college recruiters.

Drill #13: Straight-Line Dribble

Purpose:

To teach players to improve ballhandling at a high rate of speed.

Description:

Three lines with equal numbers of players on each side of the floor. Dribble ball one-third of the way across the floor and back up the same distance as fast as you can go and under control. Then go two-thirds of the way and back up one-third. Repeat until you go all the way across the floor. Then make a two-hand chest pass to first player in the other line. Then you will attack the ball like a defender, which allows the ball handler to work on a jab step and pivot. (See Figure 13-A.)

Coaching Cues:

Hand on top of ball and increase speed as much as possible and remain under control.

Coach:

Wayne Cobb is the head basketball coach at East Central University in Ada, Oklahoma. Wayne has won over 590 games in his 33-year career. His teams have won 11 conference championships and made four national tournaments, finishing as the runner-up in 1989.

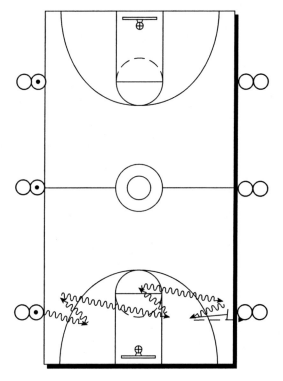

Figure 13-A
Straight Line Dribble

Drill #14: 3-Ball

Purpose:

To teach ballhandling, jump shooting and power layups.

Description:

A three-man weave from half-court against one defender (Figure 14-A). On the second pass, the middle man finishes at the basket with a shot blocker. The other two players catch and shoot jumpers at the elbows (Figure 14-B). Middle players on weave must catch, handle, locate defense and finish strong for potential three-point play. Shooters need to get feet set for a good rhythmic jumper. The defense must give an angle and make contact so there is no risk of injury.

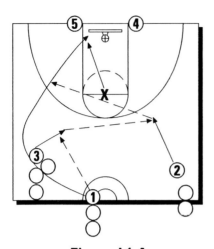

Figure 14-A
3-on-1 Weave

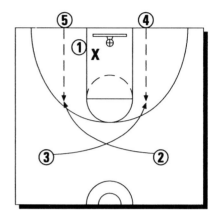

Figure 14-B

Figure 14-C
Reset Three Ball Drill

Coaching Cues:

Utilize movement and shooting fundamentals—score under pressure.

Coach:

Blaine Taylor is an assistant basketball coach at Stanford under head coach Mike Montgomery. Both are former coaches at Montana and have established the Stanford Cardinal program as one of the premier basketball programs in the country.

Drill #15: Long Pass and Dribble

Purpose:

To teach players the long hook, baseball, or two-handed chest pass.

Description:

- The squad is divided, with half the players at either end of the court, as shown in Figure 15-A. A player under the basket dribbles to the side of the lane and throws a hook, baseball or two-handed pass to his cutting teammate. The pass receiver then drives hard to the other end of the court and lays the ball up. The passer then breaks upcourt and receives a similar long pass from

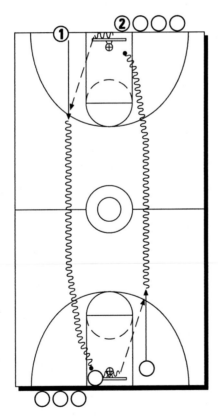

Figure 15-A

the next player in line who has retrieved the layup. After the driver lays the ball up, he goes to the end of the line at that end of the court and waits his turn to retrieve the layup shot and pass upcourt to the player in front of him.

- This drill is worked on either side of the court so that players acquire practice in making a long pass in either direction. This is a good conditioner, as well as a drill that provides long passing and dribbling practice.

Coaching Cues:

1. Lead the receiver.

2. Put backspin on the ball to keep it in the air longer.

3. Catch the ball before dribbling it.

Coach:

Jack Ramsay was a collegiate coach at St. Joseph's University (PA). Later, he coached the Portland TrailBlazers and the Indiana Pacers. He currently is a color commentator for NBA basketball with ESPN. His Portland team won an NBA Championship and he was inducted into the Hall of Fame in 1992.

Drill #16: Up-and-Under Move

Purpose:

To teach guards and small forwards a one-on-one offensive move.

Description:

- Player O1 stands one-half step above the box in the low post area. Player X1 is the defensive player and stands near player O1. Player X1 has the ball (Figure 16-A).

- Player X1 throws ball to player O1, who catches the ball, making sure his knees are bent. Player O1 turns, pivots on his left foot, squares up, faces the baseline and makes a violent pump fake, bringing the ball up to his forehead. He then takes one hard dribble with the hand furthest away from player X1 and takes the ball hard to the basket (Figures 16-B and 16-C).

- If player X1 goes for the pump fake, then player O1 ducks under. If player X1 stays on the ground, player O1 jumps in the air after a pump fake, squares in the air to the basket and shoots the ball.

Figure 16-A
Initial Set

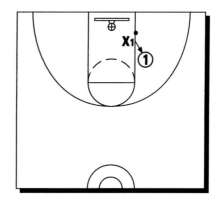

Figure 16-B
Basket Move Outside

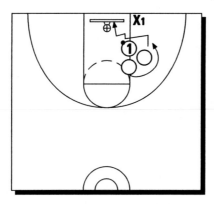

Figure 16-C
Basket Move Inside

Coaching Cues:

1. Player O1 must remember to keep his knees bent until after he makes his pump fake.

2. Players should practice this move 25 times per day from each side of the court.

Coach:

Pete Gillen is the head basketball coach at the University of Virginia. Coach Gillens'teams are noted for playing aggressive defense. Coach Gillen formerly coached at Xavier University and Providence College.

Drill #17: Posting Up

Purpose:

To show young post players how to flash to the ball and make a strong move.

Description:

Post starts opposite block and flashes across the lane with the coach hitting him with the bag. Post has to be strong and establish position on the block, feels the defender and makes a move. All the time, the coach pushes on the post player with the bag.

Coaching Cues:

1. V-cut from opposite block, setting defender up (Figure 17-A).

2. Establish position on block by using your lower body and an arm bar on the defender, with opposite hand calling for the ball (Figure 17-B).

3. Prior to receiving the ball, take a little hop and catch ball with both hands.

4. Chin the ball.

5. Squat down on defender's legs and take a look for the defender on the baseline.

6. Now they are ready to execute an offensive move.

7. Teach basic post moves (Figure 17-C).

- drop step/power

- up and under

- jump hook

Later, add a high post feeder. Low post player must seal defender and work defender toward side being defended.

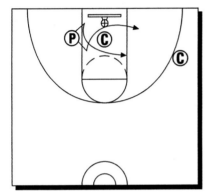

Figure 17-A
Getting Open

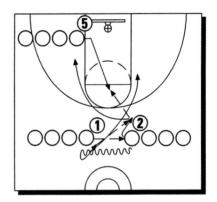

Figure 17-B
Posting Up

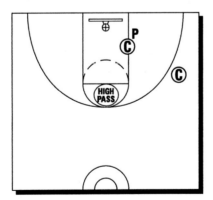

Figure 17-C
Post Moves

Coach:

Mike Amos is an assistant basketball coach under head coach Tom Oswald at the North Dakota State College of Science, a community college in North Dakota.

Drill #18: 1-on-0 Post Moves with Two Shots

Purpose:

To teach offensive post-play on both sides of the lane.

Description:

- Start with a line of post players under the basket, each with a ball (Figure 18-A). The first player passes his ball to the first coach/manager on the wing. He steps out to the block and posts up, receives the pass and makes a power move to the middle of the lane and shoots a jump shot or a jump hook. He rebounds the ball and makes an outlet pass to the other coach/manager on the opposite wing, follows his pass to the other block, posts up on the block, receives the pass and shoots a square-up (turnaround), turning to the baseline. (Figure 18-B).

- This is repeated with the following combination of moves: (1) power post to the middle; (2) square up to the middle, lift and power to the baseline; (3) power to the middle, lift up and step through; (4) square up to the middle, lift, step through to the baseline, power to the baseline; (5) square up middle, power post to the baseline; (6) square up to the baseline, lift and power to the middle; (7) power to the baseline, lift and step through; (8) square up to the baseline, lift and step through.

- Then reverse side to where the back-to-the-basket moves are on the other side and the square-up moves are on the side where the power moves started.

Coaching Cues:

1. Post up big.

2. Come to and chin the ball.

3. Make moves at game speed.

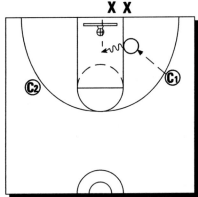

Figure 18-A
1-on-0 Post Moves

Figure 18-B
Reverse Side

Coach:

Curtis Janz has been the head assistant coach at Oklahoma Christian University for 10 years, where the OCU program has become a consistent NAIA national contender with excellent post players.

Drill #19: Squeeze

Purpose:

To teach inside players to handle the ball in traffic and score in the lane.

Description:

An offensive player is stationed on the opposite side of the lane from a coach, with two defenders located in the lane (one at the free throw line and one on the baseline), as shown in Figure 19-A. Coach says "go," and the offensive player sprints toward the coach. When the coach passes the ball to the offensive player, both defenders try to squeeze him. It becomes a 1-on-2, with the offensive player trying to score on two defenders.

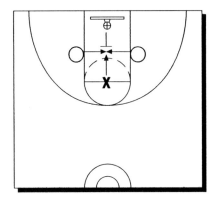

Figure 19-A

Coaching Cues:

1. Meet the pass (go to the ball), catch the ball with two hands and chin the ball.

2. Go to the basket to score—use the backboard and assume all shots will be missed.

3. Be strong with the ball.

Coach:

Dick Davey is head coach of Santa Clara University. He has a long and distinguished career as a high school coach (five years at Leland H.S., San Jose, CA), assistant coach at California University (five years) and assistant at Santa Clara (15 years with Carroll Williams). His five-year stint heading the Broncos has been characterized by West Coast Conference championships and big-game upsets. Dick's teams are well known for their execution and mastery of basic skills.

Drill #20: Developing Your Big Men Year Round

Purpose

Provide an off- and in-season improvement program for frontcourt players.

Description:

- Coaches in any sport generally adhere to the philosophy that players improve most during the off-season. The off-season gives a player the luxury of working on various dimensions of his game at his own pace, promoting self-discipline, self-motivation and self-evaluation.

- The last characteristic may be the most critical to an individual's growth as a basketball player. A player must be able to continually evaluate himself and his progress as he works to improve his game. Coaches evaluate their players each day, yet, unfortunately, players are not often taught how to evaluate themselves. Self-reflection may not be an innate skill and may therefore have to be taught by the coach.

Implementing a Plan.

For continued improvement, a player must reflect on his accomplishments and shortcomings and, with his coach's supervision, develop a plan. When an individual understands his abilities, sets goals and works within such a plan, he will inevitably develop into a better basketball player.

The off-season affords maximum time for player improvement, but the true mark of a coach and his program is how much his players develop during the season. Of course, a coach can always hide behind the belief that during the season there is not enough time to work on individual skills. However, for overall team success, it is imperative that coaches budget their practice time to include an individual improvement segment. Obviously, drills for your Nos. 3, 4 and 5 men are only one type of program that can be incorporated into your practice plans.

At Kean College, we have infused a wide variety of low post conditioning drills to improve our efficiency from 15 feet and in. The station work presented is for a 20-minute workout (50-second station/10-second rotation). On many occasions, we have consolidated the station work to a 10-minute (20-second station/10-second rotation) workout. We utilize one-half court and have access to three baskets. The court setup and explanations of the drill work are as follows (Figure 20-A):

Circuit Explanation

1. Movement in a good defensive stance—side-to-side slide while executing five types of game passes.

Chapter 1—Fundamental Drills

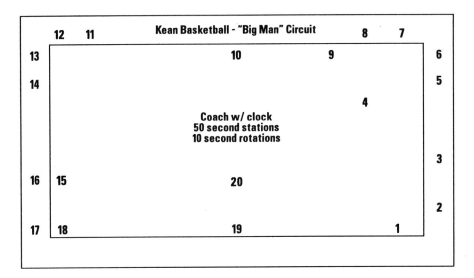

Figure 20-A

2. Against wall or bleacher, jump off two feet (quick jumps), reach with two hands.

3. Two-foot jumps, jumping jacks, straddle, box jump, single leg, single-leg box, double jumps, mix it up.

4. Big man individual skills:

   • Superman—Lane line to lane line drill. Start in outside lane, toss basketball (outlet pass) to opposite corner of backboard (above the rim), slide across lane; before crossing opposite lane line, jump in the air and catch the basketball off the board with your arms above your head. Immediately repeat drill to opposite side, etc. Make sure arms stay above the head for the entire drill—excellent rebounding drill.

   • Sikma—Toss basketball out to mid-court area (baseline moves) or foul line area (elbow moves), working on inside and outside pivots, while always keeping the basketball above your head in a ready-to-shoot position.

   • McHale—Also called an "up and under move." In the box area, from a front pivot, fake jumper, step through with same leg to the lane, shoot a baby hook. Work from both boxes and mid-lane areas.

   • Malone—Toss basketball off glass, rebound it and take it right back to the rack, constantly working on legs (quick jump) and keeping hands above head at all times.

5.   A set of 10–25 push-ups, followed by line jump (foot quickness). Find a line and do quick short jumps back and forth for remainder of station.

6.   Working on stationary shooting form. Shoot against a wall; pick a spot and shoot at it consistently while concentrating on body balance, correct form and follow-through.

7.   Defensive drill for leg strength. Great mental test also. Players sit against a wall like a "chair." Legs are perpendicular to the floor, the back is flat against the wall and hands are straight in the air.

8.   Stick four pieces of tape on floor in shape of a square. Player jumps to each piece of tape in a pattern or design. Coach varies pattern with each player. Must keep your players sharp and thinking.

9.   Football drill—Player, lying down, holds legs six inches off ground for length of station.

10.   Box drills—An excellent drill is the "power J" drill. It was developed as a multipurpose drill for improving our ability to score in the box area and lane area and to sharpen our interior passing efficiency. This drill requires three basketballs and six players. One player is in the drill and starts on a box. Two players are under the basket as rebounders, two are in each wing area (with a basketball) and another player is at the top of the key (with a basketball).

On the whistle, one of the wing players feeds the low post (hook pass), the offensive player makes a quick post move (varies with coach's input) and goes to the opposite box for another hook pass, layup. The players stationed under the basket rebound their respective basketballs and throw (outlet pass) back out to the wing on their side of the floor. After the offensive player finishes his second power layup, he touches the baseline under the basket and flashes to the middle area of the lane ("old" broken line area) for a chest pass from the player at the top of the key. He shoots a short lane jump shot and immediately follows his shot for the layup, whether he made the jump shot or missed. He must then rebound his own shot and pass (outlet pass) back out to the man at the top of the key. He immediately dives back to the low box, where he started and repeats the drill.

A player can score a maximum of four baskets with each trip. The players compete against the clock and themselves as the high scorer at the end of the drill does not run, and all the other players run the difference of their scores, with the winner in full-court sprints.(At various times, also incorporate boxing-out drills.)

11. Tie a rope to a dumbbell and pull it so the rope is taut. Have your player start his ascent up the rope "climb" with quick two-foot jumps. Once he reaches the top (or as high as he can go), have him begin his descent with the same process.

12. Same as No. 7.

13. Same as No. 6.

14. A set of 10–25 push-ups, followed by players lying on their back and shooting straight up into the air. Great drill to see if they are "hooking" or "pulling" the basketball. If the player shoots the basketball with good form, it should land right back in his open hand.

15. Using statistics, two areas are addressed: the area where the player is currently shooting the best, and the area where the player is shooting the worst (always include foul shooting).

16. Same as No. 3.

17. Stationary/speed dribbling with big ball (may use cones, etc.).

18. Stationary "wrap" drills—around head, waist, legs, etc.

19. Defensive slide drill—width of court. Not concerned with speed, but concerned with form.

20. Defensive backpedal drill—width of court. Concerned with speed and form, hands raised above head.

Skill-Specific Emphasis

The intention of this article is to promote the necessity of individual improvement in a daily practice situation. The drill work presented is comprehensive as to the skill-specific fundamentals the big people in our program are required to develop. Skill-specific drills for big men, guards, individual defense, team defense, etc., should be emphasized and utilized as needed. Obviously, we all "hide" players in certain situations, but we still need to address our players' and team's strengths and weaknesses on a daily basis in order to be successful.

Philosophically speaking, a player has to be "the best he can be" in order for the team to be the best it can be. Perhaps at the Division III level, players need more individual improvement, but at any level, either pre-practice, practice or post-practice, time should be set aside for individual improvement drill work. When incorporating individual drills into a comprehensive practice scheme, a coach is limited only by his imagination.

Coaching Cues:

Structure the program so each station provides performance feedback to the player directly. Performance feedback gives your players objective status and progress measurement.

Coach:

Michael J. Gatley was coaching at Kean College of New Jersey when this article was written.

Drill #21: Combination Passing and Shooting

Purpose:

To teach players to pass and shoot.

Description:

- Ball starts at the top of the key with 1. 1 passes the ball to 3, cutting to the basket for a layup. 1 rebounds the ball and passes to 6. 1 goes to the shooting line behind 5.

- 3, after shooting the layup, follows 6. 6 passes the ball to 7 and follows his pass behind 7. Then 7 moves to the position (top of key) previously occupied by 1. 3 passes the ball diagonally to 7 at top of key. Continue with the drill. To switch shooting sides, just change positions. (See Figure 21-A.)

Coaching Cues:

1. Bounce pass for a layup.

2. Thumbs up and thumbs down on all passes.

3. Hit the spot target.

4. Call receiver's name before passing it to him.

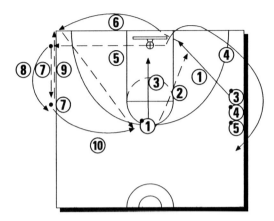

Figure 21-A

Coach:

Everett Dean was elected to the Basketball Hall of Fame in 1966, after a long and successful coaching career at Indiana University. His teams also won NCAA-1 championships.

Drill #22: Take the Charge/Go for Loose Ball/Hard to Basket

Purpose:

To teach taking the charge, aggressiveness, scoring under pressure.

Description:

All players form a single line. The defensive player takes the charge on the baseline and scrambles to his feet. The coach rolls the ball on the floor and the defender dives on the ball (Figure 22-A). After passing the ball to a coach and recovering the ball, the player takes the ball to the basket using a power layup (Figure 22-B). The manager hits the player with a blocking dummy.

Coaching Cues:

This drill allows the player to develop the courage to take the charge and develop aggressiveness in capturing a loose ball on the floor. Finally, the drill helps the player focus on making the layup during physical contact.

Figure 22-A
Take Charge
Dive on Loose Ball

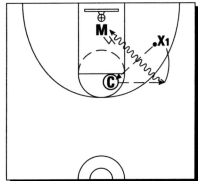

Figure 22-B
Pass-Catch-Drive-Score

Coach:

Don Lane has been the head basketball coach at Transylvania University for 23 years. He has over 450 collegiate victories and over 500 career wins. He was elected to the NAIA Basketball Hall of Fame in 1998.

Drill #23: Crestview Basketball Shooting Drills

Purpose:

To work on improving not only our offensive players' shooting skills, but also to improve on other offensive skills that go hand-in-hand with shooting: getting the shot off quicker (before the defense can react and defend our shots better); catching the ball better; making a quicker and a better pivot as the shooter catches the ball; and making better passes to the shooter (using various types of passes). Something that can also be worked on in a subtle manner is the challenge of reading how and where the ball will come off of the backboard or rim (to improve offensive rebounding). Conditioning of the players can also be incorporated in the drills. Competition against other players or other groups or against the clock or against pre-set standards is incorporated into the drills to make the drills as competitive (and therefore game-realistic) as possible. The drills are executed at a frantic pace to make the drills similar to game situations.

Description:

Every shooting drill that we use has definite characteristics. They must be as "game-realistic" as possible. They must be as "time-efficient" as possible. We would like to work on as many different phases of the game at the same time as we possibly can. We do not want to waste any time during our practice sessions. To make our shooting drills as game-realistic as possible, we must incorporate as many types of pressure as possible. We try to incorporate "success" and "competition" pressure—trying to beat other players, other groups, other opponents. The so-called other opponents can be pre-set standards and can also be the clock. Obviously, we stress accuracy in all of our shooting drills, but we also stress quantity. We continually are accelerating our rebounders, our passers and our shooters in each and every one of our shooting drills. So we have pre-set quantity AND quality standards set for each shooting drill we use. That increases the game realism, because each individual is trying to succeed not only for himself, but also for his team (or group or squad). Every shooting drill has a pre-set standard of a specific number of attempts the shooter must take as well as how many shots he should make. Again, this forces the tempo and intensity level up for each shooting drill we use.

Game realism also means rewards for the winners and penalties for the losers. None of the penalties are harsh or hard, but they are true penalties. They could be some type of a running penalty, some push-ups or sit-ups. Competing against the clock is always beneficial, because everyone has a common opponent. Using the scoreboard clock not only gives everyone a common opponent, but also a clear, visible and constant opponent. Using time limits always speeds up the shooting groups—it does not allow a shooter to take his time in shooting. We use the phrase "Be quick, but don't be in a hurry." When in a game does a shooter, a passer or any player have the luxury to take his time to go at a "comfortable speed"? By continually accelerating our players in all drills (not just shooting), we get players used to having a much quicker comfortable speed. We also want to incorporate other offensive techniques and fundamentals into each shooting drill, such as passing, rebounding, cutting, coming off of screens, catching, pivoting and, obviously, shooting. We incorporate the spots where we will most likely get those shots, as well as the types of passes we will have to use. If the coach constantly emphasizes the speed and intensity needed, other drills will naturally pick up the same speed and intensity levels that are required for those drills to be successful. Another by-product of these shooting drills can be conditioning. If everyone works at meeting the quantity and quality standards that have been set, everyone's conditioning will also improve. (Note: the numbers used are intended to more easily identify and classify the different shooting drills.)

Coaching Cues:

The locations of the passers, the defenders (when required) and the shooters vary within the drills, within the shooters, within the desires of the coaching staff. For example, if your perimeter players are the shooters in the first drills described below, you would most likely want them to be outside the three-point line. When post players take their turn as the shooters, their locations (spots and distances from the basket) would vary greatly from the perimeter players' locations. The locations of the passers should vary according to the role and the talent of the shooter. We want shooters to practice shots that they take in a game and also where they receive the pass.

Shooting Drills
(Categorized numerically)

100—"Timed Shootings" (1, 2, 3, 4 or 5 minutes) (1 + 1 min. = approx. 18 = 18)

One player is the designated passer and rebounder/retriever, while the other player is the shooter. The passer must keep track of "makes" and "misses" for his partner, so that the shooter has to concentrate on nothing but his shooting. After time has expired, the two players rotate positions and assignment responsibilities. The shot locations are determined by the location of the player's shots during games. Quantity and quality of shots are measured and recorded.

101.   (1 ball, 2 men) Off of pass—Inside Shots (1 1/2 + 1 1/2 = 27–30 shots per shooter)(70% = 21)

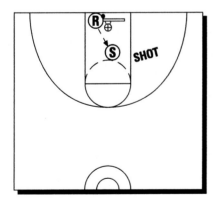

Figure 23-101

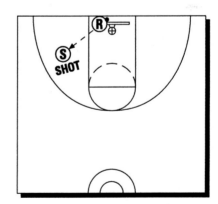

Figure 23-102

102.   (1 ball, 2 men) Off of pass—Outside Shots (1 1/2 +1 1/2 = 24–27 shots per shooter)(60% = 16)

103.   (1 ball, 2 men) Off of pass—3 Pt. Shots (1 1/2 +1 1/2 = 21–24 shots per shooter)(50% = 12)

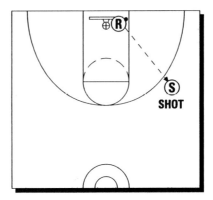

Figure 23-103

200—"Closeout Shooting Drills" off of Pass

One player is the shooter, while the other player passes the ball to the shooter. The passer then rushes out to provide a passive type of closeout defense on the shooter. The passer/closeout defender then becomes the shooter, while the original shooter follows his shot and then becomes the next passer/closeout defender. The shooter in this drill must keep track of his own "makes and misses" and NOT for his partner. The shot locations are determined by the location of the player's shots during games. Quantity and quality of shots are measured and recorded.

201.   (1 ball, 2 men and rotation) off of pass—Inside Shots (3 min. total = 38 + 38)

        A total of 3 min. should yield 37–39 shots for both shooters (70% = 26 made shots)

202.   (1 ball, 2 men and rotation) off of pass—Outside Shots (3 min. total = 36 + 36)

        A total of 3 min. should yield 35–37 shots for both shooters (60% = 22 made shots)

203.   (1 ball, 2 men and rotation) off of pass—3-point Shots (3 min. total = 30 + 30)

A total of 3 min. should yield 28–32 shots for both shooters (50% = 15 made shots)

204. (Rapid fire with 2 balls, 3 men and rotation) off of pass. Take an outside shot or a 3-pointer.

A total of 3 min. should yield 26–28 shots for each shooter (50% = 13 made shots)

Figure 23-203

Figure 23-204

300—"Closeout Shooting Drills" off of Dribble

One player is the shooter, while the other player passes the ball to the shooter. The passer then rushes out to provide a passive type of closeout defense on the shooter. The shooter makes a good (realistic) shot fake and then "scrapes" off of the rushing defender to the left (and to the right) of the defender for a predesignated number of dribbles. He drives to the basket and then pulls up to take a jump shot off of the dribble. The passer/closeout defender then becomes the shooter, while the original shooter follows his shot and then becomes the next passer/closeout defender. The shooter in this drill must keep track of his own "makes and misses" and NOT for his partner. The shot locations are determined by the location of the player's shots during games. Quantity and quality of shots are measured and recorded.

301. (1 ball, 2 men) Fake a 3-pointer, take an "outside" shot. Change directions and number of dribbles.

A total of 3 min. should yield 33–35 shots for both shooters (60% = 20 made shots)

Figure 23-301

302.   (I ball, 2 men) Fake an "outside" shot, take a power shot. Change direction and dribble.

A total of 3 min. should yield 30–32 shots for both shooters (70% = 22 made shots)

303.   (I ball, 3 men and rotation) Shot fake. I–3 dribbles, power layup versus an inside defender. Shot fake, "scrape" off def., 3 min. total = 20 + 20 + 20 shots (60% = 12 made shots each)

304.   (I ball, 4 men and rotation) Shot fake, I–3 dribbles, "drive and dish" versus "inside def."

A total of 4 min. should yield 14–16 shots for each of the 4 shooters (70% = 10 makes)

305.   (I ball, 4 men and rotation) Shot fake, I–3 dribbles, "penetrate and pitch" for a "3."

A total of 4 min. should yield 10–12 shots for each shooter (50% = 5 makes)

306.   (Rapid fire with 2 balls, 3 men and rotation) Off of the dribble, after a shot fake. Fake a "3" and take an outside shot.

A total of 3 min. = 24 + 24 + 24 (60% = 14 made shots)

400—"55-Second" Shooting Drill (3 min. total = 12 + 12 + 12)

(1 ball, 3 min. should yield 12–14 shots for each of the 3 shooters)

This drill requires three players—a rebounder, a passer, and a shooter. The rebounder works on reading the shot and grabbing the offensive rebound. He then makes an outlet pass (with proper techniques that are emphasized) to the passer, who has cut from one spot to a designated (passing) spot. The passer then makes (with proper techniques emphasized) a pre-designated pass to the shooter. The shooter has cut from one spot to his designated (shooting) spot to take his shot. The shooter keeps track of "makes and misses." After 55 seconds, the three players have five seconds in which to rotate to take a new assignment, and the drill smoothly and fluidly continues, until all three players have taken their turn at shooting, as well as passing and rebounding.

401.   (1 ball, 3 men—shooter, passer and rebounder) Off of pass (3 min. = 13 + 13 + 13)(60% = 7 makes)

402.   (1 ball, 3 men—shooter, passer and rebounder) Shot fake, 1 dribble, pull-up "J" (50% = 6 makes)

403.   55-Second Shooting Drill—"Inside Shots" versus "Bubble Defense" (2 bubble defenders, 1 shooter)

404.   55-Second Shooting Drill—"2nd Shots" versus "Bubble Defense." Shooter must follow for stick-back.

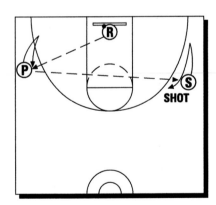

Figure 23-401

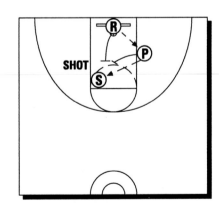

Figure 23-403

500—"Rapid Fire 55-second" Shooting Drill (3 min. total = 23 + 23 + 23)

This drill has the same format as the "3-Minute, 55-Second Shooting Drill" mentioned above, with one exception. To increase the intensity and the speed of the drill, an additional basketball is used. As soon as the rebounder passes the (first) ball to the passer, he gets ready to make a pass to the passer with the second ball. The second ball speeds up the pace of the drill dramatically for all three players involved.

501.   (With 2 balls, 3 men-shooter, passer, and rebounder) Off of the pass.

A total of 3 min. should yield 22–24 shots per shooter (60% = 14 made shots; 50% = 11 makes)

Figure 23-501

600—"Power Shots" (Left and Right Sides) (2 minutes/shooter)

These particular shooting drills are for each individual player with his own basketball. There are two players (staggered on opposite sides of the lane) at each basket. Once a player shoots from one side, the player on the opposite side shoots. After each player shoots, he goes to the opposite side. Each player keeps track of his own "makes and misses," to be recorded at the end of the drill. To add more game realism, all power shots could be shot with one player being the shooter and the other player being a defender, with football "bubble pads" used to bump and foul the shooter.

601.   "Show & Go Opposite" Drop-Step Power Moves, toward middle and baseline (20 shots)(80% = 16)

602. "Square-up, Up & Under" Crossover Power Moves toward baseline and middle (18 shots)(80% = 14)

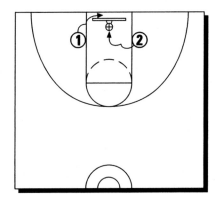

Figure 23-601   **Figure 23-602**

603. "Whirl Moves" toward the baseline and toward the middle (20 shots)(80% = 16 made shots)

604. "Dot Shots With NO Fakes" (20/make 16), 1 fake (15/make 12) and 2 fakes (14/make 11)

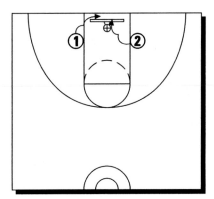

Figure 23-603

605. "Mikan Drill" and "Baby Hook Shots" (Left and right sides)

606. Duck-in to "black-line" and "rip-step through drop-step" power moves.

607. "Spin-Screen" Shots (from the Secondary Break) (2 shooters—both sides)

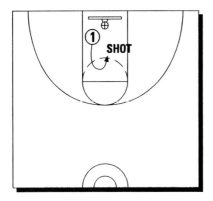

Figure 23-604a

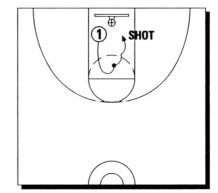

Figure 23-604b

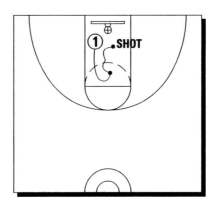

Figure 23-604c

700—"Flex" Breakdown Shooting Drills

This is a good and productive shooting drill, especially if your team runs the Flex Man Offense. You start with a line of players in the ballside corner, the ballside "block" area, the ballside "elbow" area, and the offside "elbow" area. A coach or manager starts with a basketball at the beginning of the line, located at the offside "elbow" area. The player immediately behind the coach/manager also has a basketball. The third basketball starts in the ballside corner. He initiates the drill by passing the ball to the first man in the ballside "elbow" area line, who reverses the ball to the first man in line without a ball, in the offside "elbow" area. When that pass is reversed, all of the flex action takes place, the back screen and the cut, the down screen and the cut. The offside "elbow" area line now has three basketballs. One of those passers makes the pass to his pre-designated cutter, the second man makes his pass to his assigned cutter, while the third passer makes his pass to his assigned cutter. After each of the players receives the pass to him, he must quickly catch, square up and shoot the ball at that location. On shooting the ball, he must quickly follow his shot and grab the offensive rebound (whether made or missed) and take one "stick-back" shot. This drill incorporates two screeners, two cutters off of those screens, three passers, three shooters, three offensive rebounders and the constant repetition of the offense.

701.(3 balls, 4 shooters, 1 manager) Both sides of floor. "Flex" spot-ups, 3 passing lines.

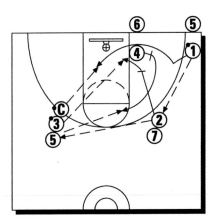

Figure 23-701

800—"35" Shooting Contest (20 shots per shooter in 4–5 minutes)

801.   (1 ball, 2 men) Should take 4–5 minutes. This drill requires that you select **five** different spots on the court (outside the 3 pt. line). The shooter takes one shot from behind the line (for 3 points); he ball fakes and takes an outside shot (for 2 points) and then ball fakes and drives for a driving "power inside

Chapter 1—Fundamental Drills

shot" (worth 1 pt). The maximum for each shooting spot on the court is 6 points (3 + 2 + 1), if all three shots are made. After the 15 shots are taken, the shooter then takes 5 consecutive free throws. A perfect score would be 35 points. The direction of the fakes and the number of dribbles taken should change often.

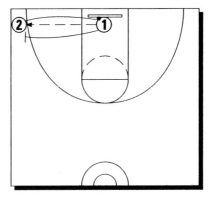

Figure 23-801

900—"Beat Michael Jordan" Shot Drill (18 shots/shooter in 5 minutes)

901.   (1 ball, 2 men) Use **six** different spots on the floor, all off of the pass. Every spot has a "3," an "outside shot" and an "inside shot." Both shooters should take about 2 1/2 minutes each. The scoring is +1 point for every made shot made and a +1 for Jordan for every shot missed. The shooter's score must beat Michael Jordan's score. A penalty could be assessed for every point below Jordan's score. Should take about 5 minutes for both shooters.

1000—"Follow Your Shot" Shooting Drill (15 shots/shooter in 3 minutes)

1001.   (3 men, 2 basketballs) Start with two passers underneath the basket. The "first passer" passes it out to the "shooter" and closes out with hands up. The "shooter" shoots and follows the shot with a "stick-back" (without a dribble, regardless of whether the initial shot was made or missed). While the first "stick-back" takes place, the "first passer" now squares up and receives a pass from the "second passer." The second passer repeats what the first passer did, while the first passer repeats what the shooter did. The shooter then repeats what the second passer did. The shooting spots can remain the same, or they can be constantly changing (Around the World). The accuracy level goals also vary for each individual. The outlet pass should not be made until the stick-back is being shot. (15 shots of both kinds per shooter in 3 minutes of drill.)

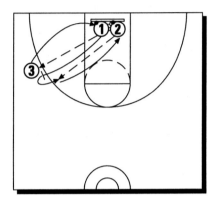

Figure 23-1101

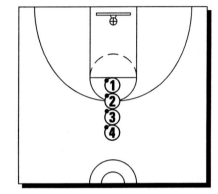

Figure 23-1201

1100—"Free Throw Swish" Shooting Drill

1101.　(4 balls, 4 men) Scoring is kept in the following manner:

　　A. A "swished" free throw, not hitting the rim, is worth "+1" point.

　　B. A made free throw is worth "0" points; a missed FT is worth "-1" points.

　　C. Should take 2 1/2 minutes for all four shooters to shoot 5 free throws.

1200—"Solo Shooting" Drill (3 minutes total = 26 shots per shooter)

1201.　Each player shoots a "J" and follows his shot to rebound. He dribbles out to the same spot on the same side of floor to take the next "J" off of the dribble or pass to himself. Goal is to take 8–10 shots per minute. Try for at least 50% made. Repeat at new spot. (1 ball per man, max. of 4 at a basket) Should take 3 minutes for 1 spot on both sides of basket for each shooter.

1300—"Free Throw Bonus Team" Drill (3 minutes total)

1301.　(12 balls, 12 men) Each player shoots a "1-and-1" bonus free throw. If the shot is made, that shooter gets another free throw attempt.

1302.   A specified number of free throws must be made. An example would be for a 12-man team to make 20 free throws. Should take 3 minutes total.

1400—"Tennessee Free Throw" Shooting Drill

(1 group of 3 men and 1 basketball). Each player takes his turn in shooting a pair of free throws, while the other two participants in the drill work on different aspects of the "Free Throw Game." This would include one player working on defensively boxing out an opponent, getting the defensive rebound, and making an outlet pass. The other player would serve as offensive competition for the defender, by attempting to beat the defense and grabbing the offensive rebound. He would then work on making the offensive "stick-back." The free throw shooter would work on quick reasons after the free throws are shot, by becoming a jump shooter on any FT misses. After two free throws, all three participants rotate to a new and different spot. After all three players have taken 5 pairs of free throws, their made free throws, the number of missed defensive box-outs and the number of made jump shots and made "stick-backs" are tallied up and recorded for later use. Those statistics can be used as a reward/punishment for individual or two-man or three-man groups. These practice stats can be weighed against pre-designated amounts. Not making those set standards

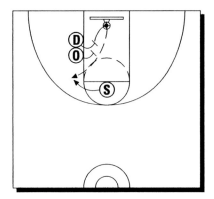

Figure 23-1401

could result in push-ups, sit-ups or some type of sprints at the end of practice, with those who "made" the standards watching. The bottom line in each shooting drill is to work not only on the shooting, but also on the shooting techniques, the pass receiving techniques, the passing techniques, the offensive rebounding techniques and as many offensive techniques as possible.

Every drill must be executed at "game speed" with "game pressures" to maximize the time and effort spent on the drills.

Coach:

John Kimble, formerly coach of Crestview High School, Crestview, Florida.

Drill #24: Nine-Spot Shooting

Purpose:

To develop the ability to shoot field goals from all angles and ranges while conditioning.

Description:

- Players execute field goal attempts from nine different spots on the floor (Figure 24-A). In a 2-minute period the player shoots nine 3's and nine 2's. A perfect score is 45 points. A player shoots from spots in chronological order.

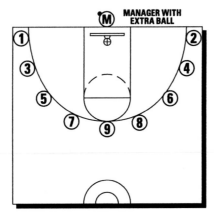

**Figure 24-A
Nine Spots**

- The format: Shoot a 3 at #1, sprint for rebound. Shoot a 3 at #2, rebound, go back to #1, ball fake, go body-to-body by defender (if there is one), one dribble, short mid-range jumper. Go to #2, ball fake, etc. Manager will only give extra ball to player if rebound bounces wildly and player has to chase it. Player must go full out in order to get the 18 shots off. Coach can jog to the different spots and give token defensive pressure or give offensive player token defense.

Coaching Cues:

1. Emphasis is on 2-point shots.

2. Go by defender "body-to-body."

3. When going from spot to spot, dribble hard with your weak hand.

Coach:

Jim O'Brien is an associate basketball coach with the Boston Celtics. He has served under head coach Pick Pitino with the New York Knicks, the University of Kentucky, and currently with the Boston Celtics. Rick Pitino has won national championships at Kentucky.

Drill #25: Team 3-Ball

Purpose:

To teach competitive spot shooting.

Description:

*   Two even groups of players split up at each end of floor. The groups will shoot from four designated spots (Figure 25-A). Fifty makes at each spot. Each group starts on the elbow (1). Next, each group starts on the wings (2), then the corner (3) and finally the three-point shot (4).

*   First group to 50 made baskets wins.

*   Each group uses three balls (Figure 25-B). Shooter follows shot and passes to player in opposite line and then goes to end of that line.

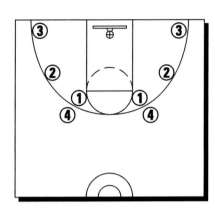

Figure 25-A
Shooting Spots:
Elbow, Wing,
Corner, 3 pt.

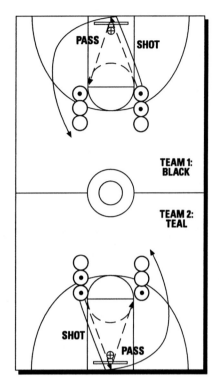

Figure 25-B
Split Ends

Coaching Cues:

1.   Quick movement, crisp passes, at game speed.

2.   Triple thrust position.

3.   Follow through.

Coach:

Mark Osowski is an assistant basketball coach with the Charlotte Hornets, under his former head coach, Dave Cowens. In 1991, Cowens was elected to the Basketball Hall of Fame for his playing career with the fabled Boston Celtics.

Drill #26: 30-Second Shooting

Purpose:

To teach shooting at game speed.

Description:

Get from point A to point B as quickly as possible (Figure 26-A). Shooting spots can vary from anywhere on the floor (Figure 26-B). Everything is quick, except the actual shooting fundamental techniques. The drill utilizes different shooting spots on the floor and emphasizess shot count being at 8 made or better. Three-point shooting will aim for 6 made (Figure 26-C).

Coaching Cues:

1.   Be quick to spot up, but don't rush shooting technique.

2.   Learn to get a rhythm in your shooting pattern at game speed.

3.   Emphasize technique, footwork, footwork with a dribble and full-court shooting at spots.

Coach:

Billy Tubbs is the head basketball coach at Texas Christian University. He formerly coached at Southwestern University, Lamar University, and the University of Oklahoma. His teams are known for their shooting and high-tempo game. His 23-year career includes regular tournament appearances and Final Four runs in both the NIT (1981) and the NCAA (1988). He was selected National Coach of the Year in 1984.

Drill #27: Triangle Shooting

Purpose:

To teach players to create as many high-quality shooting attempts as possible.

Description:

Drill #1: 3 shoots and follows shot; 2 rebounds the shot

(See Figures 26A through 26C)

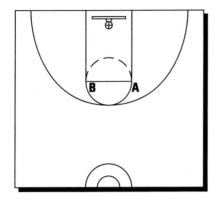

Figure 26-A
Spot A to Spot B
(30 seconds)

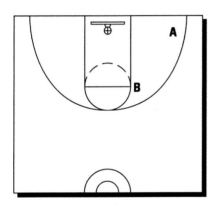

Figure 26-B
30 Second Shooting
(different shots)

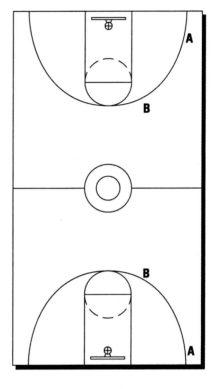

Figure 26-C
30 Second Shooting
(Field Goal)

Drill #2: 2 passes to 1 and closes out on 1

Drill #3: 1 shoots and then makes a V-cut to the top; 2 replaces 1 in the corner

Drill #4: 3 rebounds 1's shot and then passes back to 1, who has cut from the corner; 1 shoots from the top

Drill #5: 3 rebounds again and passes back to 2 in the corner; 1 follows shot; drill repeats as in step #1.

(See Figures 27-A through 27-E.)

Figure 27-A
Start

Figure 27-B
Closeout

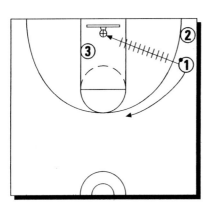

Figure 27-C

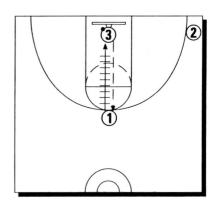

Figure 27-D
Reset

**Figure 27-E
Continuous**

Coaching Cues:

1. Game shots, game spots, game speed

2. Live-ball moves and correct shooting technique

3. Defensive closeouts

4. Block-outs for rebounding

5. Passing and receiving

Coach:

Robert Davenport is the new head basketball coach at Missouri Baptist College, following a stint at LeTourneau University in Longview, Texas.

Drill #28: Partner Shooting Drills—Using Screens

Purpose:

To teach players to simulate game conditions and work together to create game-like shots.

Description:

Coach or assigned passer works with two players—screener and cutter—to create shots in four screening situations:

- Back-Screen Flare (Figure 28-A). Player simulates coming off a back screen and flares to the corner. Overhead pass is thrown to the inside shoulder. Shooter catches with knees bent and steps into his shot. Shooter follows his shot, passes to partner and returns to original spot. Make seven shots, then rotate.

  (NOTE: Do not backpedal when flaring. Rotate your hips and run, seeing the ball.)

- Back-Screen Pop-Back (Figure 28-B). Shooter starts on the block and steps out to simulate a back screen. As cutter comes off the screen, screener steps to the ball with hands ready and fingers pointing up. Catch the ball with knees bent and immediately elevate and take the shot. Make seven shots, then rotate.

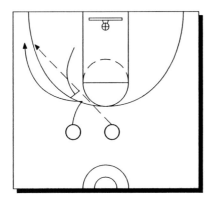

Figure 28-A

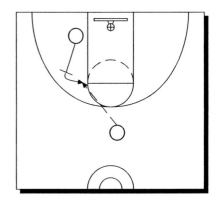

Figure 28-B

- Screen-Away Flash (Figure 28-C). Shooter simulates using a screen away by taking man away and then coming hard to the ball. Hand should be ready to receive the ball, with fingers pointing up. Catch the ball with knees bent and immediately elevate shot. Make seven shots, then rotate.

- Screen and Step-Back (Figure 28-D). Offensive player screens on ball. Ball handler comes off the screen aggressively. Instead of rolling to the basket, the screener steps back with hands ready to receive the pass. Catch the ball with knees bent and step into the shot. Make seven shots, then rotate.

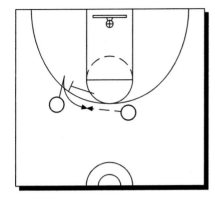

Figure 28-C

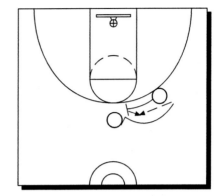

Figure 28-D

Coaching Cues:

1.   Set good screens and use them.

2.   On flares, run with vision.

3.   Be ready to shoot.

4.   Simulate game conditions.

Coach:

Billy Donovan and Donnie Jones coach at the University of Florida. Their 1999 team reached the NCAA-I Sweet Sixteen, where they were eliminated on a last-second shot by Gonzaga University. Donnie is an assistant to Coach Donovan.

Drill #29: Penetrate and Kick—2-Minute Shooting

Purpose:

To develop the capability to shoot off dribble penetration.

Description:

Coach passes ball to player. Player shot fakes and dribble penetrates into lane. As he gets into the lane, he passes out to the wing. Shooter receives ball, ready to shoot;

passer runs toward shooter to contest shot (Figure 29-A). Shooter runs down his own rebound. Both players switch lines. Drill is done for 2–3 minutes. The drill is modified to get shots from the top of the key (Figure 29-B).

Figure 29-A
Shot from Wing

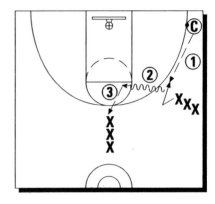

Figure 29-B
Shot from Top of Key

Figure 29-C
Shot from Corner

Coaching Cues:

1.   Good fake shot.

2.   Penetrate into lane to draw the help defense.

Chapter I—Fundamental Drills

3. Pass out to shooter.

4. Shooter ready to receive ball and step into shot.

Coach:

Steve Lappas is in his seventh season as the head basketball coach at Villanova University, where his teams have won 20 games in each of five of the last six seasons and appeared in four NCAA tournaments. In 1994 the Wildcats won the NIT Championship.

Drill #30: Accordion Shooting

Purpose:

To teach proper shooting technique and footwork.

Description:

Player begins on one side of the floor. "X" indicates dots placed on the floor. Coach serves as rebounder/passer. After shooting in first gate, player runs to baseline and then proceeds to next gate. Once player gets to opposite corner, he performs the same activity in reverse direction. (See Figures 30-A, 30-B and 30-C.)

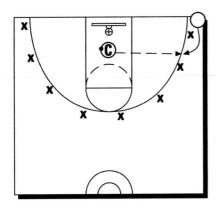

Figure 30-A

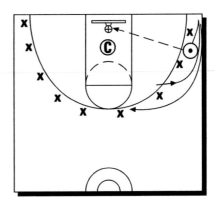

Figure 30-B

Figure 30-C

Coaching Cues:

Players work on catching low and pivoting correctly.

Coach:

Dave Magarity is the head basketball coach at Marist College in Poughkeepsie, N.Y..

Drill #31: Around the World

Purpose:

To teach players to shoot after executing an offensive fake and/or live ball move.

Description:

Catch in a triple-threat position; use a lift or pump fake. Remember to keep the knees bent, use the proper live ball move (direct drive or crossover). Go one dribble, quick stop and shoot (Figure 31-A). Then back up outside the arc, receive a pass and do it again. It takes about 8–10 shots to get all the way around the world. Partner passes the whole time we go around the world (Figure 31-B). Players will switch places at the end of an around-the-world circuit.

Coaching Cues:

1.   Catching in triple threat position.

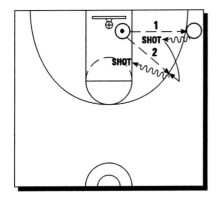

Figure 31-A
Pass-Drive-Shot Fake

Figure 31-B
Around-the-World

2.   Keep butt down on lift

3.   Square-up to basket.

4.   Follow through.

5.   Good passing.

Coach:

Dan Hays, head basketball coach at Oklahoma Christian University, has accumulated over 400 college wins and has been elected to the NAIA Basketball Hall of Fame.

Drill #32: Intensity Shooting

Purpose:

To teach players competition shooting with drills that are timed, intense and motivating.

Description:

Two years ago we came up with a positive way to work on shooting in practice that keeps players intense, competitive, and motivated and also allows us to take advantage of the three-point line. By using these drills, we have seen our shooters' range increase and their accuracy improve. During the last two seasons, we have shot 53.5 percent from the floor and have led our conference in scoring. Last year we finished second in three-point baskets, and this year we led our conference in both three-point percentage and total three-point baskets. As players see their improvement, they become increasingly motivated to continue the hard work necessary to stay sharp.

To put it simply, all we have done is to take some concepts given to players at summer camps and incorporate them into team drills. By doing these drills with intensity, you will fatigue your players so that they will be shooting under game-like conditions. Try these drills. At first, scores will be low, but as players increase their speed, quickness and endurance, scores will improve. We believe that your team's shooting percentage will improve as well.

We do not do all of the drills every day, but we do try to have two shooting sessions per practice that can last from 5 to 10 minutes each, depending on our schedule. We shoot competitively every day. We work just as hard the day before a game, as well as later in the year, although our time on the drills might be reduced to a minimum of 30 seconds. We never shoot for less than 30 seconds or more than a minute per shooter per drill. These short, explosive bursts of work help to maintain intensity and concentration.

All drills are done in pairs, and all drills are timed. Players must call out their score as each basket is made. After each particular drill or "event," each player's score is recorded (we record after both players have shot). If the drill lasts for one minute, then it will take a little over two minutes to do the entire drill, and then we record.

The player with the most baskets or points for the entire team wins that particular event and will get his score circled. For each "circle" a player gets, he receives five bonus points to his total score at the end of the day. Each individual drill is competitive and each player's score for every drill counts toward his final daily total. We run a couple of sprints for shooting after practice. The top three shooters for that day do not have to run these sprints. It's amazing what this little incentive will do to motivate.

Shooters are encouraged to shoot their outside shots just beyond the 19'9" line. Our strictly inside players do not go beyond the line. We believe that this quick, repetitive and competitive shooting grooves the shooter for the three-pointer. Players are really interested in their scores and will work hard on these drills.

The Drills

- **Hustle Shots** (Figure 32-A)—Players start under the basket, shoot a layup or a dunk, let the ball go and sprint to the free throw line. They must touch the free throw line with their hand and then go pick the ball up, shoot it from where they pick it up, leave the ball and sprint back to touch the free throw line.

- **Layups** (Figure 32-B)—Shooter starts with the ball at the short 17 right side. At the signal, he drives in with his right hand, shoots a layup and rebounds his shot as it goes through the net. He then speed dribbles out to the opposite short 17 with the right hand and then turns and drives back to the basket with his left hand, lays it up and rebounds the ball as it goes through the net and speed dribbles with his left hand to the original starting point, where he again switches hands and continues on. These first two drills really get the players working and get them ready to start their outside shooting sequence. We work very hard on these early in the year.

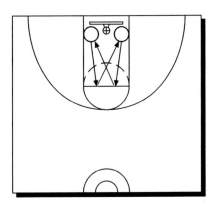 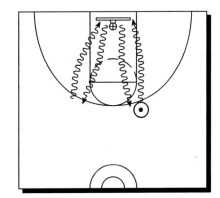

Figure 32-A   **Figure 32-B**

- **Toss and Shoot** (Figure 32-C)—Shooter starts at short 17, shoots a jump shot and gets his own rebound and tosses the ball back to the opposite short 17. He then sprints around and catches the ball on the bounce, squares up and shoots. (He is passing the ball to himself.) He then rebounds and goes to the opposite short 17.

- **Wing-to-Wing** (Figure 32-D)—Player starts at wing beyond the three-point line. Partner is under the basket as a rebounder. Shooter shoots the ball and sprints across the court to the opposite wing, beyond the three-point line. Rebounder gets the ball and passes it hard back to the shooter. The shooter shoots again and sprints back to the original side. This continues for the duration of the drill.

Figure 32-C

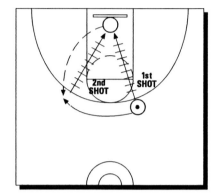

Figure 32-D

- **Toss and Shoot Wing-to-Wing** (Figure 32-E)—Player starts at red square and tosses the ball to himself at 19'9", squares up, shoots, and follows his shot. Shooter gets the ball and tosses it to himself at the opposite wing, beyond the three-point line. There is no rebounder in this drill.

- **Baseline Sprints** (Figure 32-F)—Shooter starts in the corner beyond the three-point line. He shoots the ball, sprints and recovers the made or missed shot. His partner is at the free throw line. When the shooter retrieves the ball, he passes it back out to his partner at the free throw line and continues to sprint to the opposite corner. The shooter must touch the sideline with his foot and come back to the ball, which will be delivered sharply by his partner. He catches, shoots, follows the ball and passes it back to his partner and then sprints to the opposite sideline, where he touches the sideline and comes back to the ball.

- **Close out and Shoot** (Figure 32-G)—Partner passes the ball to the shooter and then sprints and closes out on the shooter. The shooter catches the ball and goes straight up for a jump shot over the pressure. The shooter follows his shot, retrieves the ball, passes back out to his partner and closes out on him. (Players continue to change spots in this fashion until the time period is

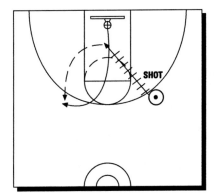

Figure 32-E

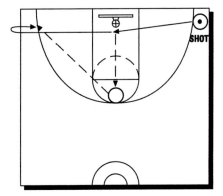

Figure 32-F

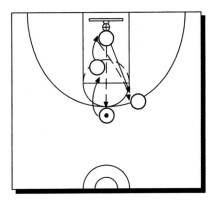

Figure 32-G

up, remembering to verbally call out each basket they make.) A good variation of this drill is to up fake before the shot and take two power dribbles either way and then shoot.

• **Spot Shooting** (Figure 32-H)—Shooter starts at the top of the key. He has spots on the floor that are worth points to him when he makes a basket from there. They are as follows: 5 points from the top of the key, 4 points for a baseline jump shot, 3 points for a jump shot from short 17, 2 points for a dunk, and 1 point for a layup (you can only shoot two layups in a row). Sometimes we do not allow more than two attempts in a row from any spot. A good score on this is over 60 points in a minute.

- **Double White Line** (Figures 32-I and 32-Ia)—This drill is so named because we have two white lines on each side of our court. In this drill, we put two groups together on the main baskets so that we would have eight players working on the main court. Everyone else uses the side baskets. The shooter stays on one side of the floor and, after each shot, must pass to the feeder, who is beyond the "double white line" on our court. The passer is about 10 feet from the top of the key. We have two shooters and two passers on each of the main baskets. The shooters are required to shoot two shots; the jumper from the short 17. Each time he shoots the ball, he must rebound it, pass it

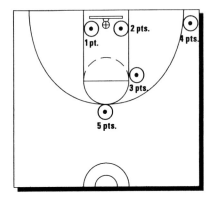

Figure 32-H

Figure 32-I

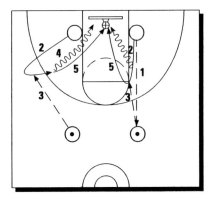

Figure 32-Ia

out hard to the feeder and move quickly to the next spot. The other pair of players on this particular basket are doing the exact same thing on their half of the court. Both shooters start at the red square and come to the ball, giving a target. One side starts by going to the wing first, and the other side starts by going to the short 17 first. In this drill, the ball starts in the hands of the passer. Shooters shoot the same two shots on the same side of the floor for the entire drill.

- **Free Throws**—We shoot two free throws at a time and shoot a total of 10 during each drill. When the coach blows the whistle, players sprint in a counterclockwise direction to the next basket on a two-man fast break. This will eliminate standing around, eliminate needless talking, and increase concentration. You can score the drill in one of two ways: (1) You can count total free throws made out of 10, or (2) you can shoot 10 free throws, two at a time, and switch positions. A "swish" is worth two points. A made free throw that hits the rim is one point, and a miss is a minus-1 point. In this way, the highest possible score would be 20 points for 10 made free throws without hitting the rim.

These are ten drills that we use. Use your imagination to do things that fit your facility and your team. We believe in these drills and will continue to use them, for we have seen improvement in our overall shooting. These concepts can readily be used by players to work on their shooting in the off-season. Since they have had this practice supervision during the season, they know what it's like to really work on their shot. The point-total concept readily lends itself to setting and achieving specific goals.

Coaching Cues:

These drills allow you to focus upon the proper execution of the fundamental skills leading to a score—footwork, ballhandling and shooting mechanics. Then emphasize taking "game shots at game spots at game speed."

Coach:

Don Frank was coaching at Rancho Santiago College (CA) when he wrote this article.

Drill #33: Charting the Shooter

Purpose:

To teach players how to discover flaws in their shooting.

Description:

Have the players shooting from the free throw area, or any other designated spot, with a person doing charting from behind the shooters. Chart players shooting free throws as to what part of the rim the ball hits or if it's a swish. We make 30 or more circles on the recording sheet and mark them as shown below:

1.   ball hits left side of rim

2.   ball hits right side of rim

3.   ball hits back of rim

4.   ball hits front of rim

5.   ball swishes

If ball goes in after hitting portion checked, we place "X" there also. We find this very helpful in working with shooting and free throws. If a person is always hitting at a particular area, we can usually show the player why.

Coaching Cues:

Use correct free throw and field goal shooting techniques. Person charting should verbally give the feedback location on each shot.

Coach:

Charles Anderson is the head basketball coach at Aquinas College in Nashville, Tennessee, where he has accumulated over 400 wins after a high school coaching career with over 400 wins.

Drill #34: Free Throws

Purpose:

To teach players to simulate game competition and shoot under pressure situations.

Description:

As a coach, you must teach your players how to concentrate and constantly challenge them. Hence, we set up drills that put them at a disadvantage or in a pressure situation.

Drill #1: Five-Point Game

- 5 points for a swish (no rim)

- 4 points when ball hits any part of rim

- 3 points when ball hits both sides of rim

- 2 points when ball hits rim three times, rattles, etc.

- 1 point when ball rolls around rim or hits backboard

- 0 points for a miss

Now the shooter must concentrate not only on making the shot, but also on *how* he puts the ball through the cylinder.

Drill #2: The Lap Game

- Divide your team into two, three, four, etc., groups.

- Each player gets one shot.

- If the first player makes his shot and the second player misses his, then the player who misses must sprint a lap.

- If the first two players make their shots, but the third misses, then he runs two laps ... and so forth.

This drill is a good game, because pressure steadily increases on the players as shots are made.

Drill #3: The Basket Game

- Each player must make a free throw at each basket in the gym consecutively, or he must start over (i.e., you can name any number you want).

This breaks the routine of the shooter and forces the players to adjust.

Coaching Cues:

1. Know how you want your players to shoot free throws and insist they shoot them that way (change unless they shoot over 80%).

2. Shoot with your legs (finish on tiptoes).

3. Follow through—elbow points to rim and hold gooseneck for count of two every time.

4. Eyes on target at all times.

5. Breathe to relax.

6. See yourself making the shot before you shoot.

Coach:

Mike Dunlap is a former head coach at California Lutheran University and in Australia. He is now at Metropolitan State College in Denver, Colorado, where his 1999 team was NCAA-II national runner-up. His article first appeared in the Fall 1989 *Basketball Bulletin*.

Drill #35: Concentrated Practice Drills for the Free Throw

Purpose:

To teach players a variety of drills to improve their free throw shooting.

Description:

Concentrated practice drills

Each player's practice session must be self-motivated and goal related.

- Shoot 100 shots (a day) to develop ritual.

- Shoot 100 shots and chart percentage made.

- Shoot for 10 consecutive shots made. Then shoot for 10 consecutive swishes.

- Keep a record of consecutive shots made and constantly challenge own record.

- Shoot one-and-one at each basket in gymnasium to improve concentration through change in perspective (different background, different lighting).

- Challenge buddy in a one-on-one situation; on a missed shot, run sprints.

- Pressure Situation: sprint from end line to end line, then go to free throw line and shoot one-and-one until you score 20 points.

- Gimmick: shoot with red, white and blue ball or tape ball into quarters to emphasize backspin.

- Gimmick: shoot with gloves on to develop and improve the feel for the ball.

- Develop a mental ritual to build concentration, which, in turn, will provide a strong frame of mind. Say to yourself, "Relaxation—Concentration—Follow-Through."

Coaching Cues:

1. Reduce unnecessary motion.

2. Hold follow-through (up-and-out motion).

3. Tuck elbow in.

4. Guide hand on side of ball.

5. Promote or turn shooting hand slightly to the right.

6. Pause two to three seconds in dip position.

7. Keep body weight forward.

8. Lock into a ritual.

9. Maintain a consistent arc.

10. Be patient with a planned program.

Coach:

Gary Palladino coached at the University of Hartford when he wrote this article for the Spring 1980 *Basketball Bulletin*.

Drill #36: Roll and Switch

Purpose:

To teach players to recognize the roll and switch, to call out "switch."

Description:

• Figure 36-A shows a defensive pick roll and switch drill. No ball is used in this drill. The players follow one after another as quickly as possible. The lines exchange positions at the end of one full run.

• The back player (B in the drill) must call the switch every time in a loud voice to designate that it is on. (See Figure 36-A.)

Coaching Cues:

1. Tell your teammate a screen is coming.

2. As the pick and roll is executed, call the switch and cover up on the new offensive player.

Figure 36-A

Coach:

Frank McGuire is a member of the Basketball Hall of Fame. Coach McGuire coached at the University of North Carolina and won an NCAA championship over the heavily favored University of Kansas team, led by Wilt Chamberlain. He also coached at the University of South Carolina and with the New York Knicks of the NBA.

Drill #37: Summer Improvement Drills

Purpose:

To teach players a drill routine that can be used to improve a variety of basketball skills.

Description:

Warm-up

- *Rope-Jumping.* One of the best ways to improve your agility, footwork and quickness. Start with a two-minute warm-up with a varied routine. Work on frontwards, backwards, crossover, alternate feet, etc. Then go for one minute and work up to 200 jumps consecutively.

- *Strength Development.* Work on building natural strength through a varied routine of push-ups, sit-ups, leg lifts, fingertip push-ups, and calisthenics.

- *Ballhandling Routine.*

   —"Ball-Slaps": Pound ball hard into the fingertips 25 times with each hand.

   —"Ball Tips": Tip the ball between your finger with your arms locked straight in front of you. Move your arms from above your head, down in front of your body, to your knees and back 10 times.

   —"Circles-Body": Start with tight, quick circles around your head, waist and knees together. Then spread your legs and circle each knee separately. Then start a quick, tight weave around each knee without letting the ball hit the floor. Each body part should be circled 10 times.

   —"Dribble-Weave": Dribble the ball using both hands around and through the legs in a weave. The ball should never be dribbled any higher than the knee. Keep your head up; do not watch the ball. Go as quickly as possible without losing the ball. Start with 10 repetitions and build to 20.

   —"Two-Ball Dribble": Dribble two balls simultaneously in a 10-foot radius. Go forward, backward and to both sides. Keep your vision up and off the balls. Work for one minute. The same emphasis as the drill above.

Improvement Drills

Drills are designed to be done in groups of three with a short break between each group to shoot foul shots. The workout is designed to fit a lot into a short period of time (one hour maximum). Drills are to be done as quickly as possible without losing execution of the fundamental skill.

• *Agility/Quickness* (30 seconds each). Count the number of touches each day and work to improve.

—Quick Feet: Jump with both feet over the line as quickly as possible. Maintain good balance (Figure 37-A).

—Quick Feet across the Lane: A player shuffles from one side of the lane to the other. Touch outside the lane before returning (Figure 37-B).

Figure 37-A
Quick Feet

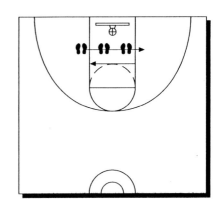

Figure 37-B
Quick Feet Across the Lane

•*Continuous "Hook" Shots.* Start with a right-handed hook, then cross over the left side without the ball hitting the floor or dropping below the shoulders. Keep two hands on the ball for the shot and use the backboard. Explode off the left foot for the right-handed hook and off the right foot for the left-handed hook. Another name for this drill is the "Mikan Drill."

Chapter 1—Fundamental Drills

- *Dribble Zigzag.* A player with the ball uses a change-of-direction dribble the length of the court in a zigzag fashion— three dribbles in one direction, then pivoting and crossing over into the other hand. The head should stay up with vision off the ball, and the ball should stay knee height or lower (Figure 37-C).

—Break for Free Throws: Shoot three sets of "one-on-ones." If you make the first shot, you get a second. On all made shots, go get the ball and reset on the line for next shot; if missed, sprint to ball, make a layup, sprint back to the line.

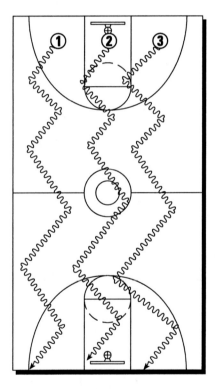

Figure 37-C
"Mikan Drill"

Chapter 1—Fundamental Drills

- *Power Layup.* The ball is thrown against the backboard, and the player jumps as high as possible to rebound the toss. As the player lands on both feet, on balance, he gives a good "shot" fake and goes strong to the basket to score, using the backboard. Keep both hands on the ball and alternate from one side of the basket to the other. Ball is kept above the shoulders (Figure 37-D).

- *Contest and Pivot—Defensive Slides.* The player assumes a low stance position and slides according to Figure 37-E. At each pivoting point, the player should "open" up and then close back into the original contesting position.

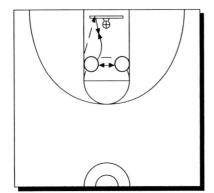

Figure 37-D
Power Layup

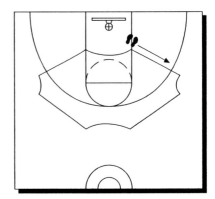

Figure 37-E
Contest and Pivot
Defensive Slides

- *Full Court Layups.* Player dribbles full speed down to the basket, shoots a layup with his off hand, takes the ball out of the net, then goes full speed to the other basket. His goal is to make four baskets in 30 seconds (Figure 37-F). Break for foul shots. Same routine as before.

- *Rim Touches.* Player jumps with both hands over his head as high as he can go. His goal is to touch the rim, but a younger player may have to start with the net as his goal. The player jumps continuously off of two legs and no step for 30 seconds. He records the number of "touches" each day so that he can check his progress. Excellent drill to help develop a higher vertical jump.

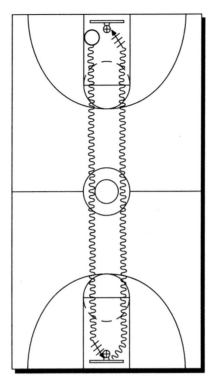

Figure 37-F
Full-Court Layups

- *Offensive Drive Moves.* The player starts with his back to the basket, facing out onto the court. The drill starts with the player making a "flip" pass to himself about 20 feet from the basket. He then goes and catches his own pass with a two-foot jump stop. We want the player to pivot into a "Triple-Threat Position" off of his left foot, facing the basket. The player should make a six-inch "foot fake" at the basket, then go into his drive. We want the player alternating between the "strongside" drive and the "crossover" drive into the left hand.

- *Consecutive Jump Shots.* The player again starts from the same position as in the previous drill. In this drill, the player pivots right into his jump shot. He rebounds his own shot and changes the spot of each shot. The player is working against the pressure of time to see how many shots he can make in 30 seconds. By doing this, the player is working on "Game Shots at Game Speed."

To conclude the workout, the player goes to the line for his foul-shot routine. To add conditioning, we want the players to do a full-court sprint (down and back) for each missed free throw in this segment.

No One Is Beat

No one is beat 'til he quits

No one is through 'til he stops

No matter how often he drops

A fellow is not down 'til he lies

In the dust and refuses to rise

Fate can slam him and bang him around

And batter his frame 'til he's sore

But he never can say that he's downed

While he bobs up serenely for more

A fellow's not down 'til he dies

Nor beat 'til no longer he tries.

—Edward White II

Coaching Cues:

After selecting drills designed to address specific needs and weaknesses of players, they should then be taught how to do the skills properly and quickly. Give them ways to self-assess their status and progress.

Coach:

This excellent article on drills for off-season improvement first appeared in the Spring 1989 *Basketball Bulletin*. It was authored by Steve Steinwedel, who, at the time, was head coach at the University of Delaware.

Drill #38: 1—4 Zone Press Breaker

Purpose:

To advance the ball safely into the frontcourt.

Description:

Provide/use diagrams (Figures 38-A through 38-F). Drill against all zone pressure defenses.

Coaching Cues:

1. Meet passes.

2. Maintain angles.

3. Keep proper spacing.

4. Read defense.

5. Keep someone behind ball at all times.

6. Do not be concerned with 10-second call.

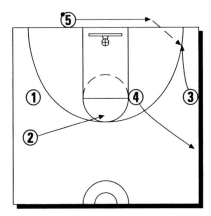

Figure 38-A
Entry Pass
Five can run endline
and pass

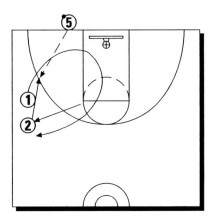

Figure 38-B
Clean and Replace Move

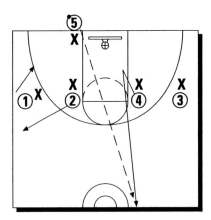

Figure 38-C
Full Denial Option

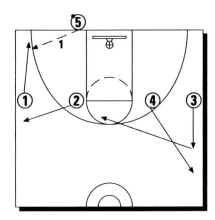

Figure 38-D
PG Entry

Coach:

Lynn Nance, was most recently the head basketball coach at Southwest Baptist University. Lynn has coached at Iowa State University, the University of Kentucky, St. Mary's University, and the University of Washington. His all-time coaching record is

293-216, and he guided Central Missouri State to the NCAA-II Championship in 1984. He has been inducted into the SBU and the Central Missouri State Halls of Fame.

Figure 38-E
First Option
Return pass and
swng ball

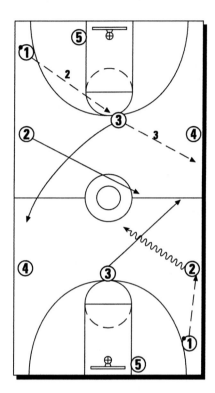

Figure 38-F
Third Option-Sideline

Drill #39: "3-on-O" Early Defense

Purpose:

To teach players to improve the following: passing on the move; jump stopping; catching the basketball in triple-threat position; making the entry pass (post); and making a strong layup to the basket.

Description:

- Player #3 (post) throws the basketball to the glass and rebounds.

- Player #1 (guard) calls for the outlet pass.

- Player #2 (guard) runs hard (full-court) to baseline.

- #1 dribbles down the floor and passes to #2.

- #3 follows and posts up (coach), using sealing technique.

- #2 passes back to #1 (top of the key), #1 entries to #3 (post). #3 takes up hard.

- The "3-on-O" drill continues on the other side of the floor, coming back.

Coaching Cues:

1. Strong rebound/chinning the basketball.

2. Strong outlet pass.

3. #1—jump stop plus hard takeoff.

4. #2—receive the basketball in triple-threat position.

5. All three players run the floor hard.

6. #3 sealing baseline when basketball is on the wing.

7. #3 sealing outside when basketball is on the top.

8. #1 making a solid/hard entry pass.

9. #3 using both hands to receive the basketball, plus keeping both hands raised up.

10. #3—DO NOT dip the ball.

11. #3—no dribble.

12. #3—go up strong.

In the "3-on-O" drill, the shots can be taken from (a) the corner by #2 player (shooting guard); (b) top of the key by #1 player (point guard); and (c) on the block by #3 player (post), after entry pass by #1 or #2 (see Figure 39-A).

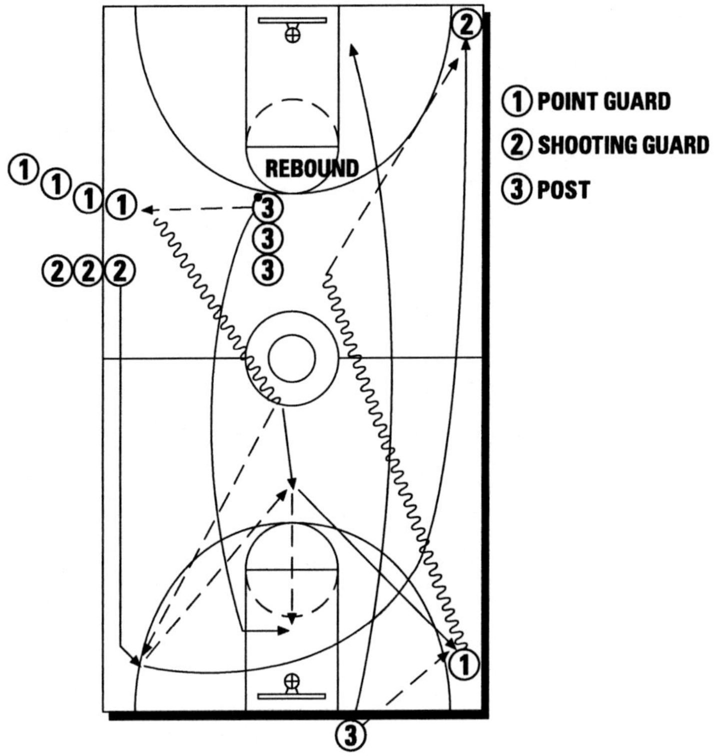

Figure 39-A

Coach:

Bob Hoffman is the head basketball coach at the University of Texas (Pan American) in Edinburg, TX. Previously, he coached at Oklahoma Baptist University, where he took the Bisons to six consecutive NAIA tournaments, as well as to national prominence. Before that, he coached Southern Nazarene University's women's team to the NAIA-I National Championship in 1989.

Drill #40: Fast-Break Inception

Purpose:

To teach rebounding, outlet passing and filling the lane.

Description:

- Two players shoot from 18 to 25 feet, corner-to-corner passing the ball from one to the other in order.

- #2 players line up on end line and come out one at a time as far as the foul line to face shooter who is allowed to shoot. As the shot is taken, the facing player executes good rebounding footwork and techniques, retrieves the rebound.

- A #3 player, stationed in the middle of the court, moves to a position along the side line for the pass, depending on which outlet pass is thrown. Right rebounds (from the shooter's viewpoint) are passed out to the right sideline; left rebounds go to the left sidelines; center rebounds go the left sideline, and shots which are made are quickly taken out of bounds and fired inbounds on the second or third step. After the pass is released, the passer follows as speedily as possible in the same lane to which he passed the ball. He stops at center in early drills; later he goes the court length for lay-up shooting, taking the feed pass from the outlet pass receiver, who has dribbled to the center lane and to the free throw line. New players move to position for continuation of the drill. (See Figure 40-A).

Figure 40-A

Coaching Cues:

1. Angle jump to the basket.

2. Chin the ball.

3. Front turn on outside foot away from defense to outlet the ball.

4. Quarter turn in the air (away from the defense) after the rebound is captured.

5. Make pass to the outside shoulder of outlet player.

6. Outlet player calls rebounder's name.

Coach:

John McClendon is a member of the Basketball Hall of Fame. John was a most successful basketball coach at Tennessee State University, Cleveland State University, and the NBA's Denver Nuggets. His legendary fast break teams at Tennessee State won three NAIA National Championships.

Drill #41: Rebound and Break

Purpose:

To teach passing, catching, and running lanes.

Description:

Ball is thrown off glass to simulate rebound—outlet #4 to #1. #3 fills middle, #2 runs/sprints wide, as seen in Figure 41-A. Rebounder trails middle to touch opposite free throw line, becomes middle man. Outlet passes to middle, stays wide, and rebounds opposite end. Middle man receives pass from outlet, passes without dribble to #2 wing spring for layup. Then middle peels opposite pass to become layup wing. Wing who shoots layup (#2) trails slowly to become outlet. #5 or next player on sideline becomes new outlet. Four players begin, and a fifth is added for one trip down the floor. The player who lays the ball in at the end of the floor of origination (A) is out and goes to the end of waiting line. (See Figure 41-B.)

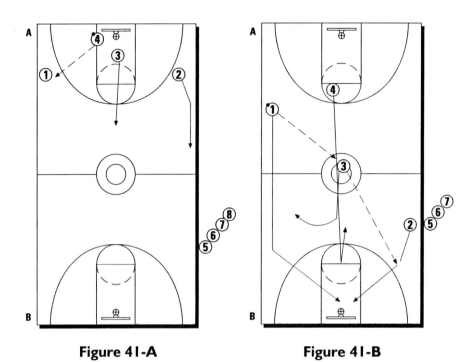

Figure 41-A   **Figure 41-B**

Coaching Cues:

1. Sprint lanes—get out and run.

2. Catch the ball.

3. Snap the pass.

4. Finish.

5. Ball does not touch the floor.

Coach:

Derek Allister has been the head basketball coach at Stephen F. Austin since 1996, after coaching at the high school and collegiate levels.

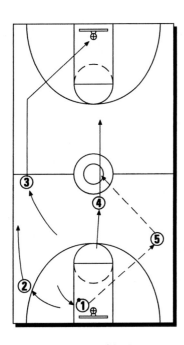

Figure 41-C

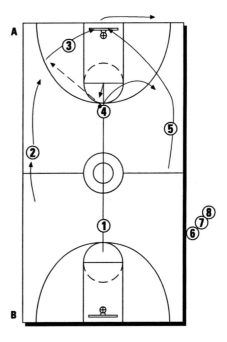

Figure 41-D

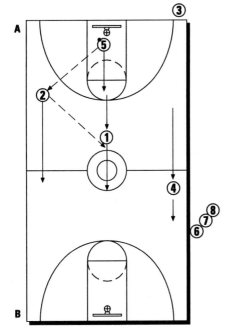

Figure 41-E

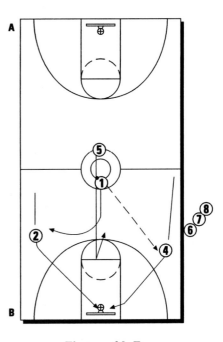

Figure 41-F

Chapter 2—Drills for Offense

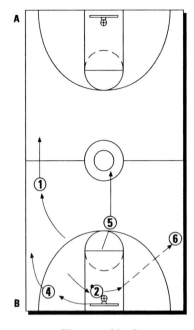

Figure 41-G

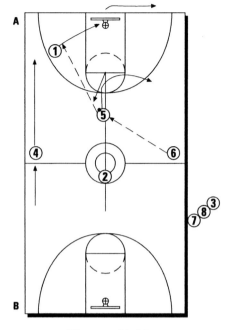

Figure 41-H

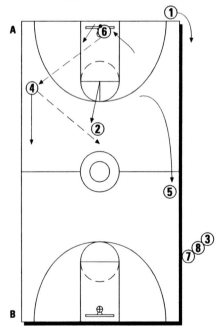

Figure 41-I

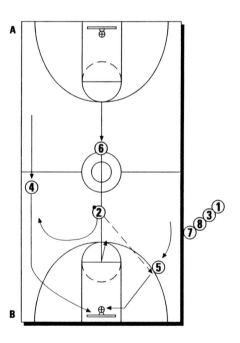

Figure 41-J

Drill #42: Fastbreak in 2s

Purpose:

To teach players to outlet and fill a wing on the fast break (defense to offense transition).
(See Figure 42-A.)

Description:

Two lines, one in the lane and one on the wing, free throw line extended.

- A player tosses the basketball off the glass and makes an outlet to the wing.

- The wing will advance the ball up the middle of the floor while the outlet man fills the wing.

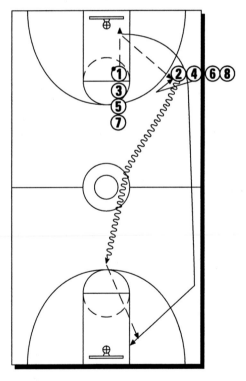

Figure 42-A
Post Break in Two's

Chapter 2—Drills for Offense

- When the middle man hits the top of the key, he will quick-stop and hit the man cutting to the basket for a layup. We tell the wing man to make his cut to the basket when he hits the free throw line extended.

- We will do the same thing on the way back, but both players will change roles.

- We do this drill with a layup, bank shot, three-pointer, and a pass back to the middle man after he makes a jab step away and comes back to the ball.

- We do this on both the right and left sides of the floor for a total of 16 trips up and down the floor.

Coaching Cues:

1. Chin the rebound and pivot outside.

2. Catch, turn, and look before you dribble.

3. Get wide on the sideline to extend the defense.

4. Quick-stop at the key.

5. Cut at the free throw line extended and cut in above the block.

6. Run hard in transition.

Coach:

Brett McDaniel is in his third year as the head basketball coach at York College in York, Nebraska. Prior to becoming head coach at York College, he served as assistant basketball coach at Oklahoma Christian University for three years.

Drill #43: Celtic Fast Break

Purpose:

To condition and teach ballhandling, passing, rebounding, and footwork.

Description:

- X1 throws ball up to backboard and rebounds for outlet pass to X6. X1 then takes one dribble to clear traffic and makes an air pass to X6 streaking toward basket (Figure 43-A).

- X1 rebounds, one dribble, air pass to X6, who dribbles to opposite foul line. X6 gathers and makes an air pass to X1 for jump shot on wing (Figure 43-B).

- Next, same concepts for X6, only bounce pass to X1 for driving layup (Figure 43-C).

- Next, X6 gathers and passes to X1, who drives to basket but gathers for draw and kick jump shot for X6, who slides to open slot (Figure 43-D).

- Same thing is happening on the other side.

- 30—60—90—120 seconds each segment.

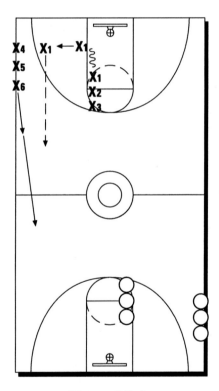

Figure 38-A
Wing Layup

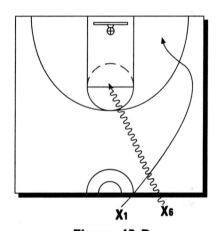

Figure 43-B
Middle to Wing

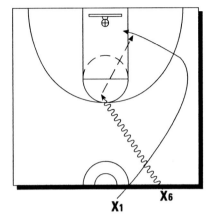

Figure 43-C

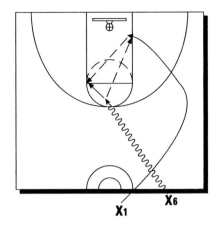

**Figure 43-D
Penetrate and Pitch**

Coaching Cues:

1. Rebound with hands high.

2. Footwork on outlet pass.

3. Good passing.

4. Run lanes hard and wide.

5. Emphasize good stopping skills.

6. Crisp passing.

7. Good spacing.

Coach:

Brock Brunkhorst was an assistant basketball coach under Rick Majerus at the University of Utah. The Utah program under Majerus advanced to the Final Four in 1998 and has become a perennial NCAA contender, while winning the Western Athletic Conference Title regularly.

Drill #44: Eleven-Man Break

Purpose:

To teach appropriate passing techniques, decision-making on the break, and basket defense against the fast break.

Description:

1, 2, and 3 take the ball down against 4 and 4. 6, 7, 8, and 9 are in the outlet spots at their respective ends of the court. 10 and 11 form the defensive tandem at the opposite end. When the shot is taken from the three-on-two situation, the three offensive men and two defensive men all go after the rebound. Whoever gets it—3, in this case, as shown in Figure 44-A—passes to the nearest outlet—6, in this case—who takes the

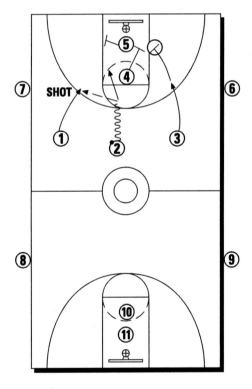

Figure 44-A

ball to the middle. The other outlet man and the rebounder form the outside lanes in a three-man-break situation, advancing the ball on 10 and 11 at the other end. As soon as the shot is taken (only one shot is allowed, and then the ball goes the opposite way), the three offensive and two defensive men go after it, with the man getting the ball joining the two outlet men going the other way, as shown in Figure 44-B.

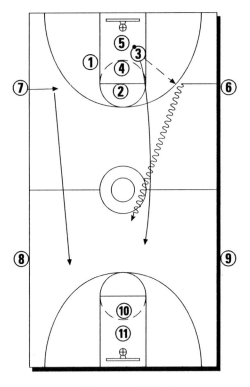

Figure 44-B

The four players who fail to capture the ball, move to either the defensive spots or the outlet positions. They decide which among themselves. There are no out-of-bounds in this drill, and if a defensive player intercepts a pass, he takes it the other way with the two outlet men. If one of your players comes up with the ball three or more times in succession on a consistent basis, you have a guy who really wants to play.

Coaching Cues:

1. Focus on fundamental passing and catching skills.

2. Stop the ball on defense.

3. Use good outlet passing.

Coach:

Bob Knight, who formerly coached at Army, is the head basketball coach at Indiana University. He was inducted into the Basketball Hall of Fame in 1991. He is the winningest coach in the history of Army and Indiana basketball.

Drill #45: Standard Break

Purpose:

To teach ballhandling and passing while moving at full-court speeds.

Description:

- 5 retrieves the ball off the backboard, and 2 and 3 come to meet the first pass. In this example, the pass is made to 2. 3 breaks crosscourt and receives the next pass in about the center of the court. 1, who has gone downcourt and into the basket, receives the next pass from 3. All players cut behind the player they pass to. 4 breaks down the other side of the court and may go into the basket or straight down to the end of the court to take the defense out of the way. 5 stays directly behind the ball as a trailer and safety man and goes into the center for rebounds.

- 1 and 4 rebound on their respective sides if a shot is taken, and 2 and 3 come out as safety men. The play may go to either side. (See Figure 45-A.)

Coaching Cues:

1. Lead the receiver.

2. Look ball into hand.

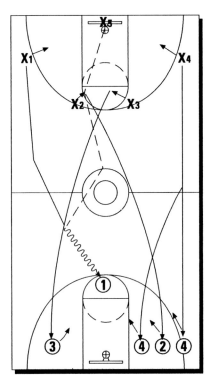

Figure 45-A

Coach:

Howard Hobson coached at Oregon and Yale. He was elected to the Basketball Hall of Fame in 1965. His Oregon "Tall Timbers" team won the first NCAA-I tournament. This drill exemplifies the drills used since the advent of the fast-break style of play in basketball.

Drill #46: Sideline Break

Purpose:

To teach players to fast-break up the sidelines.

Description:

2 finds that defense makes pass to 3 impossible, so he passes to 1 and cuts behind him

to end of the court. I passes to 3, who continues cutting hard ahead of I. 3 may pass to 2 or 4 or give ball back to I or may dribble on in or may bring in trailer man; on all breaks, man with ball has two men ahead who he may pass to if open—one immediate trailer and one safety trailer—in addition to his option of dribbling. Rebound assignments are the same. There are many variations to the fast break, but these will give a general idea of proper organization with safety and rebound plan. (See Figure 46-A.)

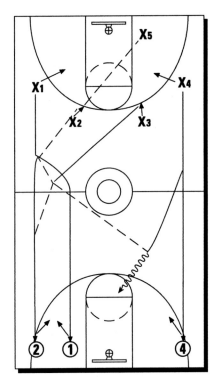

Figure 46-A

Coaching Cues:

1. Read the defense when starting and running the fast break.

2. Keep lanes wide.

3. Lead the receivers.

4. Look the ball into your hands.

Coach:

Howard Hobson coached at Oregon and Yale. He was elected to the Basketball Hall of Fame in 1965. His Oregon "Tall Timbers" team won the first NCAA I tournament. This drill exemplifies the drills used since the advent of the fast-break style of play in basketball.

Drill #47: Fast-Break Repeat

Purpose:

To teach players to accurately pass to a moving target and catch the ball while performing cutting movements.

Description:

- Divide the players into five separate groups. Each group forms a line. The first member of each group participates in the drill. The five front men are lined up equidistant from each other along the baseline, facing the opposite basket. One player is directly under the basket, with two players on each side. The outside players should be in the vicinity of the sidelines. As the five front players of each line commence the drill, the players who have been second in line assume the front of the line. At the successful conclusion of the drill, the participants move to the rear of another line.

- It is a pass-and-cut drill, with passer always following his pass to the outside, and the receiver (pass and go behind two players) always moving toward the middle of the court in his reception. The first pass is always made by the middle player of the five participants. The receiver is the close player on either side. The pass should always be to the closest player, without allowing players to be passed up. All passes are received in the middle area of the court, not in the vicinity of the sidelines. Dribbling is not allowed. The ball should always be progressed upcourt with a pass. Players shoot the layup as they approach the basket at the end of the court. After they have shot, they must quickly reassemble in five lanes and return back down the court. (See Figure 47-A.)

Coaching Cues:

1. Keep lanes equally spaced from sideline to sideline.

2. Lead the receiver slightly.

3. Thumbs up to thumbs down on each pass.

4. Repeat as many times as the coach wants; may set target goals (e.g., 10 baskets in a row).

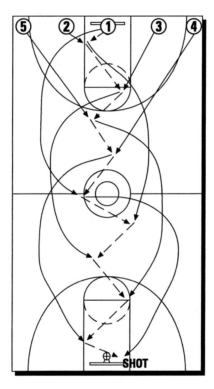

Figure 47-A
Repeats–Five player

Coach:

Pete Newell and John Bennington coached at the University of California, Berkeley, and Michigan State, respectively. Newell's California team won the NCAA-1 championship, and he was elected to the Basketball Hall of Fame in 1978. This drill, made famous by Newell, was the original defensive slide drill used in some form by most coaches today.

Drill #48: Hi-Lo Post Drill

Purpose:

To teach post players to work together.

Description:

Place the coach and two managers on wing as passers (Figure 48-A). Post players 2-on-2 trying to score, catching it only in the high or low post. Ball starts at top of key. The ball can be fed to the posts from the top or by the managers on the wings to the high or low post. Once the offensive player contacts the ball, it's "live" 2-on-2.

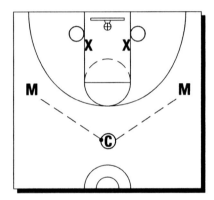

Figure 48-A
High-Low Set
Cross Screen
High-Low Cuts

Coaching Cues:

1. Seal the defender.

2. Utilize post moves.

3. Work together.

4. Be patient and aggressive.

Coach:

Rus Bradburd is an assistant basketball coach at New Mexico State University under the legendary Lou Henson. After a prominent career at Illinois, he returns to New Mexico State where he formerly coached the Roadrunners.

Drill #49: Sureness 3-3

Purpose:

To teach offensive players how to respond to changing defensive tactics in the half-court.

Description:

Offense must complete ten passes on half-court, versus the defense who can do anything (Figure 49-A). The defense can switch, trap, deny, etc. Offense should learn to work versus switching defense (Figure 49-B). Drill stops when ten passes are completed and/or when defense gets the ball. Offense then goes to defense.

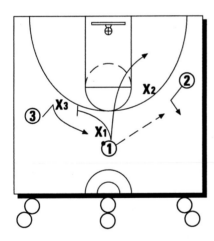

Figure 49-A
Sureness 3-on-3 Set

Figure 49-B
3-on-3 with cuts
and screens

Coaching Cues:

1. Catch and square up.

2. Meet all passes.

3. Use dribble.

4. Spacing.

5. Read ball screens (screener step back to ball).

6. Be two-handed players.

Coach:

Dick Bennett has been coaching basketball for 35 years. He is the head basketball coach at the University of Wisconsin, with back-to-back NCAA tourney appearances. Prior to coming to Wisconsin, he coached at Stevens Point, where his teams were perennial NAIA national contenders. He is recognized as a superb teacher of fundamentals and team play.

Drill #50: Zone Special–Call It Down

Purpose:

To create a perimeter shot against the back side of a zone defense.

Description:

- #1 dribbles deep enough to play with forwards coverage while looking at #3 posted, as seen in Figure 50-A. #2 must come almost to wing to receive pass (stretching the coverage from #1. #4 drops weakside into a stack with #5.On pass to #2, #3 cuts baseline corner away.

- #2 must attack the free throw line and read weakside to #3, coverage of lob to #5, duck to #4 and 3 point to #3 (Figure 50-B)

Coaching Cues:

This zone special is an example of a 5 on 5 team drill where players must be taught to execute properly and quickly while "reading" the defenders. Drill 5 on 5 until all options become automatic.

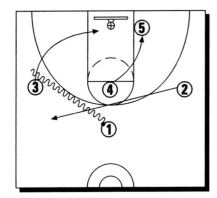

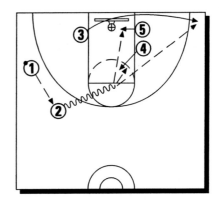

Figure 50-A
Zone special out
1-3-1 Set

Figure 50-B
Lob/Dunk or
Corner Three-Point

Coach:

Don Holst is the head basketball coach at the University of Montana after serving as an assistant for eleven years.

Drill #51: UCLA's Offensive Cutthroat

Purpose:

Teach players 3 on 3, 4 on 4 offensive and defensive half-court skills under gamelike conditions.

Description:

- Usually played half-court with 3 - 5 teams of three or four players (see Figure 51-A).

- If 3 on 3, then three lines under basket; if 4 on 4, four lines under basket.

- Offensive team should start in point-wing-wing alignment.

- Coach controls game with whistle and verbal instructions and commands. "Offense off if no triple threat, Offense off in no cutting to basket," etc.

Ball must be thrown back to coach after every basket and after every change of possession.

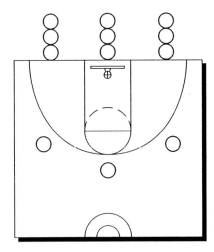

Figure 51-A

- Once coach gives ball to offensive team, that is signal for defense to run on court.

- Offense must follow certain rules. These include:

  - perimeter players must always be in triple threat position once they catch ball.

  - passer must do one of three things

  - cut hard to basket, put head under basket, turns to find open spot;

  - screen away; and

  - screen on the ball

    (Teaching progression should follow this order.)

  - when a player is trying to receive a pass and is denied, he should back cut that pressure to the basket.

  - number of passes before a shot - lay-ups always supersede any number of pass rules.

- number of dribbles rule - no dribbling is a great way to teach cutting and screening.

- give extra points for offensive rebounds.

- Coach should be very demanding on execution of the rules.

- The concepts of spacing, cut and replace, back cutting pressure, push-pull, and screening need to be taught and emphasized (see Figures 51-B and 51-C).

- If a team scores, they stay on court. Play to a certain score (3, 4, 5).

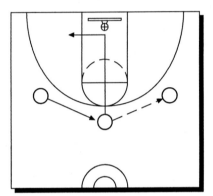

Figure 51-B

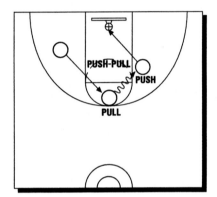

Figure 51-C

- If the offense violates one of the rules, turns the ball over, or misses a shot, they run off court to end of line. The defense will now go to offense and a new defensive team will get ready to run on the court.

- The ball must be thrown back to the coach quickly on all baskets and change of possessions. It does not matter who gets ball back to coach, as long as it gets there quickly with a good pass.

- Players must run on and off court.

- No arguing with coach or referee.

- Players on same team should talk to each other when waiting to get on court. Encourage each other and talk about what they need to do better.

Coaching Cues:

See Description. Coach should emphasize specific fundamental skill principles_select an emphasis of the day.

Coach:

Steve Lavin took over the fabled UCLA basketball program in 1996, after Jim Harrick was dismissed, and led his team into the NCAA I tournament. He is noted for his emphasis on fundamental skills.

Drill #52: Competitive Continuous Action Three-on-One Drill

Purpose:

To teach passing the ball accurately between player under controlled speed.

Description:

- Three lines of players are formed at each end of the floor. Those in the middle lane become defensive players while those in the two outside lines become offensive players. This makes it possible to keep a continuous three-on-one situation going at all times. The middle player rebounds and tosses to one of the side players cutting toward the sideline. The ball is passed or dribbled to a player in the middle area where it is advanced by passing not more than once, to either side man and back to the middle player who dribbles to the defensive player. He than fakes with his head and eyes and makes a low bounce pass to either side man for a lay-up shot.

- The defensive player recovers the ball and passes out to one of the two players who have just come from the outside lines to a position on the floor ready to go the moment the ball is captured by the defensive player. The two offensive players who just completed play move to ends of lines to await their turn again. The defensive position is filled each time by a player from the middle line who should move up near the center of the floor ready to retreat when opposed by three men breaking toward the goal he is defending. See Figure 52-A.

Coaching Cues:

1. Bend well forward at the waist to be in a position to make a low bounce under the arms of the defender.

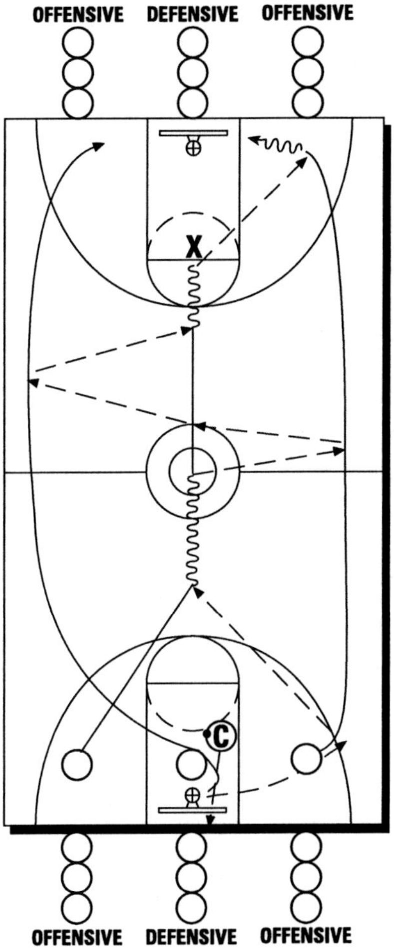

Figure 52-A

2.   Middle player comes to a quick stop at the free throw line after a veer dribble to make the defender commit.

Coach:

Jay McCreary was the basketball coach at Muncie Central High School in Muncie, Indiana, and later at Tulane University. His teams were known for their fundamentals.

3

DRILLS FOR DEFENSE

Drill #53: Butler's Man to Man Defensive Checklist

Purpose:

To develop a defensive practice/preparation plan.

Description:

- There are only a few ways to score (or create good shots) in basketball. Everything else is a combination of those few ways. If your team is prepared to defend those basic points of attack then you will be successful. Listed below are the offensive attacks we feel we must be able to stop: (1) transition; (2) dribble penetration; (3) post up; (4) off-ball screens; (5) on-ball screens (Figure 53-A); (6) basket cuts; (7) offensive rebounding; (8) screen the screener plays; (9) out of bounds plays; (10) shooter with great range and shot fakes; and (11) preventing the 3 pointer in late game situations. Each of the eleven areas must be broken down and practiced over and over.

- The coach must decide how his team will defend the various plays. Then he must drill that method into the players head until they react as the play begins to develop, not after the play has created an offensive advantage. For example, you may decide to defend the on-ball screen by hedging with the screener's defender, having the ball defender go over the screen and then the screener's defender recovers to his man after the ball defender assumes control of the ball (Figure 53-B). The other three help defenders "zone up" temporarily until the two principal defenders recover.

• The coach develops a drill or a series of drills to teach and reinforce this defensive strategy. As the players become confident with this strategy, they become prepared to face this challenge at any time in any play. This confidence allows them to face any team or any play that would use this attack.

Figure 53-A
Screens on Ball

Figure 53-B
Hedging the Screen

Coaching Cues:

Adapt to your system.

Coach:

Barry Collier has been the head basketball coach at Butler University, his alma mater since 1989. His teams have made two NCAA tournament appearances and two NIT appearances. He has served as an assistant coach at the University of Idaho, University of Oregon, and Stanford. He has been MCC Coach of Year in 1991 and 1997.

Drill #54: Shuffle and Slide

Purpose:

To teach players how to effectively move their feet in the defensive stance.

Description:

- Player stands under the basket in a defensive stance. He shuffles up to the midpoint of the foul line.

- Player then slides to his right until he reaches the end line.

- Player then shuffles to the halfcourt line.

- Player then slides to his left until he reaches the opposite end line.

- Player then shuffles backward until he reaches the foul line extended area.

- Player then slides to his right until he reaches the foul line.

- Player then shuffles backward until he is out of bounds. See Figure 54-A.

Coaching Cues:

1. Player should slide in his stance, keep his palms up, and avoid crossing his feet.

2. When shuffling, the player should keep one hand up and the other hand down for balance.

3. It is important that the player pick a point to focus his eyes on at all times.

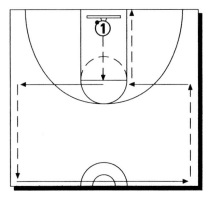

Figure 54-A

Coach:

Mike Krzyzewski is the head basketball coach at the Duke University. Coach "K"'s teams have won the NCAA Championship and appeared in the Final Four many times. His teams are noted for playing pressure defense. He is a past president of the NABC.

Drill #55: 1-on-1 Full Court Defense

Purpose:

To teach players to apply fullcourt defensive pressure, to force, and to contain opponents in the full court.

Description:

- This is a comprehensive drill in which we work on individual fullcourt pressure defense. Team members will partner up with each other. Generally, we will match the quickest two team members together and proceed accordingly with the rest of the players. We will eventually change the pairs so that one partner will have to work against a quicker player. Nonetheless, we like to have the guards face each other for the most part because that is who they will have to face in the press. Note that we only work on one side of the court and that the coaches "give help" at their stations along the boundary. This is to emphasize the PRESSURE-FORCE-CONTAIN principles in our press.

- By the time the offensive player advances the ball into the front court he has the option of passing to the coach at the top of the key and posting up. Thus, oftentimes we will work on post defense (and offense) out of this. This is an all-out, one-on-one drill which is approached with a great deal of enthusiasm and intensity by our players. That enthusiasm carries over into our corresponding drills and our press execution. See Figure 55-A.

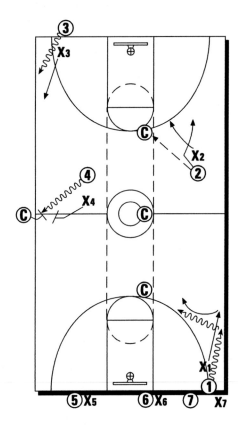

Figure 55-A
1-on-1 Full Court

Coaches Cues:

1. Short, choppy steps.

2. Keep your head, ahead of the offense.

Chapter 3—Drills for Defense

3. Turn the dribbler–force to use other hand.

4. Keep hand in passing lane.

Coach:

Tom Moore is the assistant basketball coach at the University of Connecticut under Jim Calhoun. Jim Calhoun was the head coach at Northwestern University before building the great Husky program. Under Coach Calhoun the Huskies won the NCAA Championship in 1999 and he was named the National Coach of the Year.

Drill #56: 1-on-2 Alley Drill

Purpose:

To teach players to trap in the fullcourt defense.

Description:

- This is a recognition drill where we can work on the most important things we must teach all of our front-line and second-line players. We need our front-line guys to ball pressure, dictate to a sideline, and also contain the man. Second-line guys must be able to play "cat and mouse," read when to trap the ball, and close traps hard.

- A coach inbounds the ball to a guard. X1 must pressure him and force him sideline. We teach our front-line defenders to split the inside foot of the ball handler with their feet, which will help force the ball sideline. X2 is matched to a man in the alley near midcourt. He stands slightly inside the line of the ball with his shoulders open slightly toward the sideline. As the ball is dribbled up the alley, X2 fakes at the ball taking one step up and two steps back, waiting to spring the trap. Our rule is X2 should come to trap one he senses the ball handler's head is down and he is getting out of control. Once he decides to come and trap, don't let him change his mind. Stay committed to getting the trap. We may also have some situations in this drill where X2 decides not to come and trap because he feels the dribbler never gets out of control.

- For the purposes of the drill, we have a coach inbound the ball we tell the second-line offensive player to move up the floor in relation to how the ball handler advances the ball. If they throw over our trap or split if off the dribble, the drill stops and the next group replaces them. See Figure 56-A.

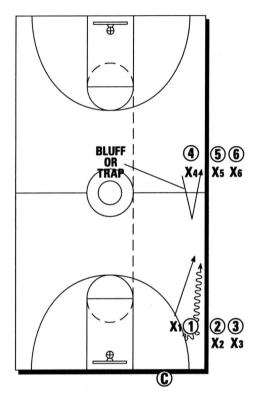

Figure 56-A
1-on-2 Alley

Coaches Cues:

1. Occupy the dribbler (pressure).

2. Keep the lead hand in the passing lane.

3. Keep the follow hand in the crossover lane.

Coach:

Tom Moore is the assistant basketball coach at the University of Connecticut under Jim Calhoun. Jim Calhoun was the head coach at Northwestern University before building the successful Husky program. Under Coach Calhoun, the Huskies won the NCAA Championship in 1999. In the process, Calhoun was named the National Coach of the Year.

Drill #57: Scramble Defense

Purpose:

To find the open man in offensive transition and to develop the capability of performing transition defense.

Description:

As seen in Figure 57-A, the coach starts the drill with the ball and passes to any offensive player (02). The coach then calls out one or two numbers (X5). 02 dribbles the ball as

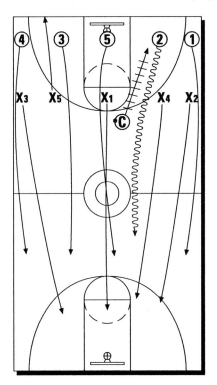

Figure 57-A
Scramble Defense

01, 03, 04 and 05 sprint to offense. 02 can pitch ahead to open players. X1, X2, X3, and X4 all sprint back to defense to protect the basket and stop the ball. The man whose number was called by coach (X5) must run and touch the baseline before sprinting back to defense.

Coaching Cues:

1.   Offense attacks in transition–finds the open man.

2.   Defense sprints back and protects the basket.

3.   Defense communicates and "scrambles" to let the offense stabilize.

Coach:

Jerry Green is head basketball coach at the University of Tennessee. Previously, he coached at the University of North Carolina-Ashville and the University of Oregon. His 1999 team advanced to the NCAA tournament.

Drill #58: The Bulldog Pride Drill

Purpose:

The Bulldog Pride Drill is designed to serve as an individual defensive drill that works on defensive techniques and skills in addition to helping create a tough hard-nosed attitude for every defensive player. The drill gives our players the opportunity to compete at a high intensity level. It can also be employed as a conditioning drill. As a rule, we also incorporate some offensive work into the drill. The offensive fundamentals and techniques that we work on in this drill are the three types of dribbling that our players are asked to use: "behind-the-back" dribbling, "between-the-leg" dribbling, and "front-crossover" dribbling.

Description:

The Bulldog Pride Drill can be conducted in a number of different ways, including the following:

•   The drill is started with offensive restrictions for two important reasons. One reason is to allow the defense an opportunity to succeed before making the drill more difficult and more "game-realistic." The second reason for giving offensive restrictions is to force the offensive players into working on specific ball-handling techniques on which the coaching staff feels that the team or individuals need to improve. Most players only like to work on the "successful" parts of their game. To make these players more well-rounded offensively, this drill has them work on the weaker parts of their game also. This approach also gives the defense a better chance for success.

- One way of making the drill more difficult for the defense (and therefore more "game-realistic") is to lengthen and widen the dribbling area. At the beginning of the drill, it can be shortened and narrowed to promote success for the defenders. As the defenders master the skills and techniques, the drill can be made more challenging and game-realistic by expanding the offensive dribbling area and letting the offensive players work on their stronger facets of ballhandling.

- When the drill is eventually advanced to using the full length of the court, the drill can then be expanded into the many different defensive techniques being applied during the course of the Bulldog Pride Drill.

Among the defensive techniques that can be incorporated into the Bulldog Pride Drill are: 1) taking the charge; 2) defending a "killed dribbler"; 3) defending a cutter (on a give-and-go situation); 4) boxing out a shooter (off of the dribble); 5) recover after the dribbler has beaten the defender; 6) diving for loose balls (closing out on a potential driver/jump shooter); 7) defending against an "on-the-ball" screen; 8) defending against an "off-the-ball screen"; 9) helping out on a teammate's man and then recovering onto his own man; 10) sprinting out of a "trap" situation onto his own man; 11) "wolf" deflecting from behind and getting ahead of the dribbler; 12) defending and pressuring a killed dribbler; and 13) jump-switching onto the new dribbler.

These and other defensive scenarios can be practiced at the very beginning and at the very end of the dribbling area. Different situations can be used every time at the beginning and at the end of the dribbling area.

Coaching Cues:

For the overall administering of the Bulldog Pride Drill, the defensive techniques that are to be emphasized in the Bulldog Pride Drill should be taught to the players first before they are stressed. Once they are introduced, these techniques can be practiced and worked on, in this and other defensive drills.

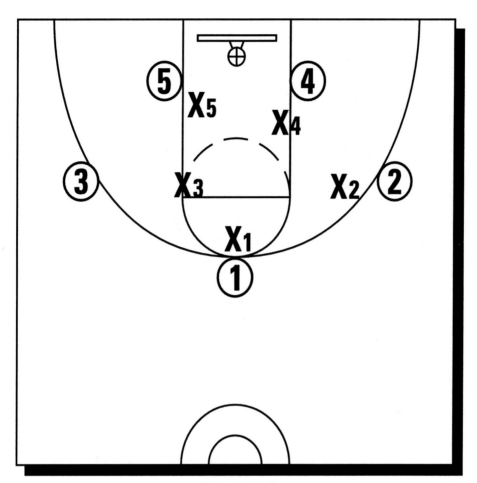

Figure 58-A
Bulldog Pride Drill

The drills above are examples of the different "defensive trips" that a team can work on during succesive repetitions. The coach should organize different combinations daily. Changing the combinations daily decreases boredom, forces players (both offensively and defensively) to listen to new instructions and forces them to concentrate on the new instructions. Mental concentration and physical intensity are a vital part of this defensive drill.

On the first trip down the court, the dribbler and the defender can create a situation where the defense must defend the new dribbler after he has received (a make-believe) skip-pass. The defender starts in a "pistol" stance and then closes out on the new dribbler. The defender now zig-zags down the dribbling area until the dribbler gets to the end of the lane, where the defender then draws an offensive charge on the dribbler.

On the first repetition. The dribbler can simply put the ball into the chest of the defender to establish the physical contact required to initiate the offensive foul. There does not have to be any other physical contact between the two players, thus decreasing the risks of injuries to either participant. When the ball has made the contact with the defender, the defender pushes off on his heels, falling to the floor. In drawing the charge, the following points of emphasis should be stressed to the players: 1) protect the groin and chest area by locking the arms in front of those two areas; 2) push off backward with the heels at the exact moment of contact; 3) tuck the chin; 4) try to slide on the tail on the floor; 5) raise the legs up into the chest area to protect from the offensive player landing on the defender; and 6) grunt out an "ugh!" to help the official make the call. The drill then continues with a new pair of players. The first pair of players go to the end of the line and switch defensive-offensive roles.

The second trip could begin with the main defender starting as a "one-pass-away", off-the-ball defender. The "dummy dribbler" should dribble into the gap of the two defenders. The main defender then "helps" (to stop penetration) and recovers to his original man as his offensive opponent receives the pass. From there, the defender uses the proper "push-push-push" and "drop-step" techniques as he zig-zags down the dribbling alley. When the dribbler reaches the far baseline, he kills his dribble. This action causes the defender to defend a "killed dribbler."

On the second repetition. The major points that should be highlighted in defending a "killed dribbler" are: 1) stepping up hard into the dribbler and forcing the potential passer to put the ball over his head or to turn away from the hard defensive pressure that is being applied. This act takes away the majority of the potential pass receivers that passer has (and remember that the passer has only five seconds to find that open receiver and make the pass to him); 2) crossface with the hands and don't allow the passer to bring the ball back down to waist or chest level; and 3) yell "work! work! work!" and pressure the passer as much as possible.

On the third trip down the defensive lane, the defender is still working on the proper techniques with his feet and his hands. The proper stance is stressed with the proper "push" technique of the feet/legs. The "dig hand" and the "extended hand and arm" techniques are constantly reinforced. The third trip can be initiated with one or two "dummy-screeners" ball-screening the defender.

On the third repetition. The defender must feel for the screen and go over the top (ballside of the screen) and hustle to stay or get ahead of the dribbler. The zig-zagging action would then continue. After turning the dribbler several times down the dribbling alley, the dribbler passes the ball to a coach or manager who is standing near the midcourt line. As soon as that pass is made, the dribbler-passer becomes a cutter. He makes a very hard "give-and-go" cut toward the end of the alley. The defender has to become a defender against a receiver (instead of a dribbler). The defender should "jump to the ball" and "match hands and belly-buttons." He should yell "Help!" and snap his head and look down his new "long-arm." The dummy passer should force a pass to the give-and-go cutter.

The fourth trip could start with an "off-the-ball" screen on the original defender. He should go "ballside" of the screen, skinny and slide through with a "long-arm." The defender should go full speed, but allow the pass (for the sake of the drill). Once the pass is completed, the dribbling and the defensive zig-zagging start all over down the dribbling alley. At the end of the fourth trip, the dribbler jumps up to simulate a jump shot off of the dribble.

On the fourth repetition. The defender defends against the shot by: 1) not leaving the ground until the shooter leaves the ground; 2) extending the hand (nearest the ball) and arm as high as possible; and 3) front-pivots into the shooter and boxes out the shooter. The defender should maintain contact on the shooter for 3 seconds before quitting.

On the fifth trip down the floor, the dribbler is allowed a two-step advantage on the defender. The defender must realize that he is beaten, pivot and open up, get the correct pursuit angle and sprint to a spot ahead of the advancing dribbler. He then must get in front of the dribbler and be "squared up" on him, knowing that the dribbler will most likely try to change directions. He should anticipate another defensive change of direction.

For the fifth repetition. The "point of teaching emphasis" we use at this time is to tell the defense they are there physically, but mentally they are already drop-stepping toward a new direction by the dribbler. The dribbler then continues "zig-zagging" down toward the far baseline. At the end of the trip, the dribbler has again been forced to kill his dribble. When that happens, the dribbler rolls out a ball for the defender to dive after.

Chapter 3—Drills for Defense

Obviously, this exercise is definitely a defensive drill. The drill, however, can be enhanced by having the dribbler working with both hands on the various types of dribbles the coaching staff allows. The head should stay up, with the body in a semi-crouch, dribbling quickly but not in a hurry. The various dribbles used could be any or all of the following: 1) the front crossover; 2) the between-the-legs dribble; 3) the behind-the-back dribble. The coaching staff could instruct the dribblers to use specific dribbles to improve upon, or a combination of them to work on offensive improvement.

The more emphasis and excitement the coach can generate and demonstrate in this drill can be extremely motivational to the players. A coach must remember that intensity is a valuable ingredient of a successful defense. Players can be better aware of what constitutes appropriate intensity levels by seeing and experiencing intensity from the coach in practice, as well as in the games.

Defensive "Pride Drill" (Starting Situations)

A.   Positioning

B.   "Closeout" from a skip-pass

C.   Downscreen

D.   Ballscreen

E.   Help-n-recover

F.   From a beaten position

G.   "55 Soft" defensive action

H.   "Jump Switch" action

I.   Sprint out of trap to the dribbler

J.   "Wolf! Wolf!" to become a "Container"

K.   From a "Stalker" to become a "Container"

Finishing Situations

A.   Boxout a "shooter"

B.   Versus a "Give-n-Go Cutter"

C.   "Work! Work!" on a "killed dribbler"

D. Take the charge

E. Trap a new receiver

F. Live "1-on-1" action

The dribbler must zig-zag, finally force the defense into the "paint", and then shoot the ball. He must then get an offensive rebound for a "stickback." When the defender gets the defensive rebound, he then must "dribble outlet" the ball until the "new" defender "turns" him at least one time.

G. Live "1-on-1" action

The offensive dribbler must try and beat the defender, using both boundary lines, regardless of how wide or narrow they are. The dribbler should use both hands with his head constantly up looking at the rim. He should be using the various types of dribbles at his disposal.

Countless combinations of "starting and ending" situations can be utilized. Mixing these combinations up helps eliminate boredom and complacency of the players. They are forced to listen and concentrate on remembering the many different defensive scenarios that the coaching staff lays out for them. The variety of scenarios can not only enhance the players' level of concentration, but also help traise their level of play.

Coach:

John Kimble, formerly coach of Crestview High School, Crestview, Florida.

Drill #59: No Hands or "Hell" Drill

Purpose:

To improve team defensive fundamental movement and positioning techniques.

Description:

•   Five-on-five team defense at quartercourt with your hands behind the back (see Figure 59-A)

•   After 30 seconds, defense uses their hands and must not allow the offense to score.

- After the turnover or rebound, the defensive team makes the offensive transition (5-on-0) to a score. The original offensive team remains at their basket preparing to play offense again (Figure 59-B).

- After the transition basket is made, the team sprints back on defense (no hands for the first 30 seconds). The coach is at halfcourt with a second ball and can throw it to the offensive team at any time (Figure 59-C).

- This sequence is repeated 3-5 times. If the offense makes a lay-up in the first 30 seconds or scores at any time, the defense starts all over again.

- Goal: The defensive team stops the offensive team 3-5 consecutive times.

Figure 59-A

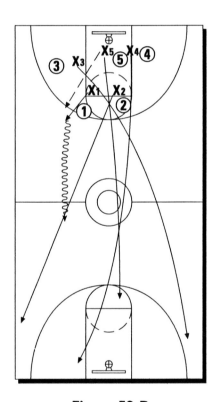

Figure 59-B

Coaching Cues:

Follow all defensive principles: ball-you-man, jump to the ball, fronting cutters, fighting through screens, etc.

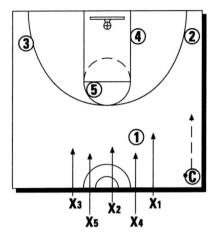

Figure 59-C

Coach:

Larry Hunter is the head basketball coach at Ohio University (8 years) and has won both the pre-season NIT, and the Mid-American Championship, while taking his teams to the NIT and NCAA tournaments.

Drill #60: Hands-Up Drill

Purpose:

To teach players to concentrate and apply the use of their feet and legs in the proper pressure defensive stance, while adhering to the proper defensive movements from that stance.

Description:

The procedure of this drill is to disperse the squad throughout the court surface, allowing for sufficient room of motion. The players should be approximately five feet apart. Each player assumes a normal defensive — stance-knees flexed, either foot extended, either arm raised, with the other arm parallel to the floor. The flexed knee and the upright hand and arm are strongly emphasized in the course of the drill. Four commands of movement are issued: right, left, forward, and rear. The directional changes of movement are varied to discourage anticipatory motion. The tempo of

Chapter 3—Drills for Defense

movement is changed constantly also. All commands should be clear and loud. A constant reminder of the correct arm position and bent knee encourages proper reaction. When the arms become leaden, the legs will stiffen and the tendency of the player is to let up when this reaction sets in. Vocal urging by the coach will help him resist the temptation.

- The first hands-up drill lasts five minutes. The length of the drill is increased slightly each day. By the end of the first week, the players should be able to manage eight minutes of the drill without a stop. Four minutes are spent with each hand raised. The load is increased to fourteen minutes by the end of the second week. In the concluding, or third, week the time is increased until twenty minutes of continuous motion are completed.

Coaching Cues:

Raise arms on commands only.

Coach:

Pete Newell and John Bennington coached at the University of California-Berkeley and Michigan State respectively. Newell's California team won the NCAA I Championship, and he was elected to the Basketball Hall of Fame in 1978. This drill, made famous by Newell, was the original defensive slide drill used in some form by most coaches today.

Drill #61: Bounce and Move Defense

Purpose:

To teach quickness and foot speed in player-to-player defense.

Description:

Basic defensive footwork, using bounce and movement footwork, are employed to increase explosive first-step technique. In the three stages, players will:

- bounce up the floor (like jumping rope); keep hands active, stay low, fire the feet (Figure 61-A).

- bounce and move. Use short choppy steps.

- bounce and slide, not just slide on defense. The goal is to bounce bigger and quicker.

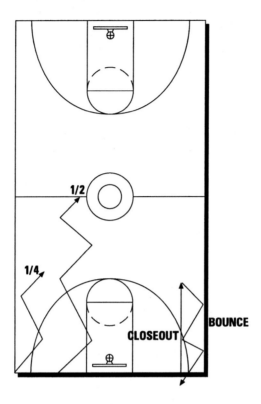

Figure 61-A
Bounce and Move
1/4, 1/2, 3/4, Full Court

Coaching Cues:

1. Keep butt down.

2. Look at target (midsection).

3. Use active hands.

4. Bounce up the floor.

Coach:

Jeff Dunlap is an assistant basketball coach at Loyola University in Chicago under Larry

Farmer. Jeff played at UCLA, and coached at the College of the Canyons, Quincy University, and Cal State University. Larry Farmer has coached successfully at UCLA and internationally, after playing in the fabled UCLA program.

Drill #62: One-Man Shell Drill

Purpose:

To develop the capability of executing defensive footwork, closing out, and recovering on a dribbler.

Description:

- Defensive player comes out under the basket with quick feet and in a defensive stance. In Figure 62-A, defensive player stands under the basket in a defensive stance with quick feet. When the coach yells "defend," the player goes out to defend the ball channeling the offensive player to the baseline. On the first pass to the top, the defender plays defense at a high angle after jumping to the ball with a palm in the passing lane. On the second pass to the opposite wing, the defender goes to helpside and plays the middle. On the third pass to the coach or manger, the coach/manager yells "shot" and the defender must close out with a hand up and then arm bar and box out

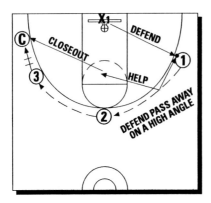

**Figure 62-A
One man shell
with close-out.**

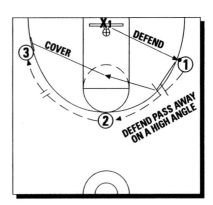

**Figure 62-B
One man shell
with cover.**

Chapter 3—Drills for Defense

- In Figure 62-B, the defender works on covering the offensive player after he/ she picks up the dribble. The first two passes are the same as Figure 62-A. The only difference is on the second pass the offensive player runs from helpside to cover and seal the shoulder of the offensive player after he picks up his dribble.

Coaching Cues:

1. Defending the opponent.

2. Jumping to the ball at a high angle.

3. Using proper footwork to close out.

4. Coach calls out where the ball is: (1) defend on wing; (2) ball at top, jump to the ball; (3) ball on opposite wing, get into helpside; (4) close out or come to cover and seal shoulder.

Coach:

Mark Morefield is an assistant basketball coach at Valparaiso University under Homer Drew. Drew has built Valpo into a nationally recognized program with an Elite Eight NCAA tourney appearance in 1998.

Drill #63: One-Man Shell

Purpose:

To teach all aspects of position defense (denial, help and recover).

Description:

One coach and four players.

- Figure 63-A. The coach begins the drill with the ball at top of the key. The defensive man starts in a one-pass-away denial. Defender extends the passing lane, denying the pass and defending the backcut (defender must make contact and decrease space between him and offense on the backcut) as offense #1 "V" cuts to get open (can only cut from wing to block). Make defender deny 3-5 cuts by the offensive player (emphasize staying low with arm extended, foot one step above offense).

167

Figure 63-A
One Pass Denial

Figure 63-B
Helpside Rotation
"2 Passes Away"

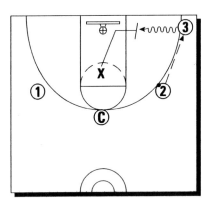

Figure 63-Ca
Backside Rotation
"3 Passes Away"

Figure 63-Cb
Recovery/Closeout

- Figure 63-B. The coach makes a pass to the opposite wing. The defensive man must jump to the ball and slide into the helpside position. The defender must be open to man and ball, and have first foot on midline (imaginary line extending from directly underneath goal, dividing court in half). Offense #2 holds ball for approximately a two-count.

- Figure 63-Ca. #2 then passes to #3 in corner, who immediately drives the ball baseline. The defender must drop (place inside foot on baseline) and take a good angle for backside help (rotate-charge is optional). Offense #3 keeps driving until he is cut off (defender back to basket) — no shot.

- Figure 63-Cb. #3 then passes to either the coach or #1 (passing to coach and then to #1 produces best timing; no cheating by players). The defender opens up and slides to recover (short and low!) as #1 drives when he catches ball. The defender takes angle to force #1 baseline out of middle (tell #1 to try to drive middle). #1 and defender go one-on-one (three-dribble limit and no jump shot off pass for offense–must drive); concludes with shot and blockout.

- One-man shell can progress into three perimeter defenders and a post defender as seen in Figure 63-D, 63-E, and 63-F. This situation has more 3-on-3, 4-on-4 situations.

Coach:

Mike Schrage is an assistant basketball coach at the University of Mississippi, where Rick Barnes is the head coach. The Ole Miss program is noted for aggressive defense.

Figure 63-D
Position Defense

Figure 63-E
Baseliner Drive

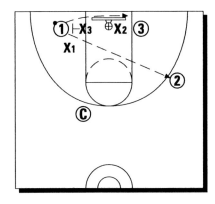

Figure 63-F

Drill #64: Contest and Interchange

Purpose:

To defend against a screen and to rotate defensively at the same time.

Description:

Identify strongside and weakside. Coach with ball can throw to either side of the floor. If down screen is on the weakside, the screener's defender must open up and let the cutter's defender through (Figure 64-A). If ball is thrown to the ballside wing, the perimeter player may drive baseline and force the weakside defense to rotate and help (Figure 64-B). Figure 64-C shows a downscreen on the strongside.

Coaching Cues:

See description of fundamental on-the-ball and off-the-ball defensive maneuvers.

Coach:

Jim O'Brien is the head basketball coach at Ohio State University, where he led the Buckeyes to a Final Four appearance in 1999 and was selected as NCAA I Coach of the Year by the NABC. He formerly coached at Boston College in the Big East.

Figure 64-A

Figure 64-B

Figure 64-C

Drill #65: Defensive Breakdown "Pick Drill"

Purpose:

To teach players the capability of playing team defense while learning to avoid and negotiatie screening situations.

Description:

- Offense begins with the point guard with the ball out front, two wings, and two posts on the block (three out, two in), with defenders on each of the five offensive players. (Posts can also start on the wings, guards on the blocks.) Players on the wings screen down on the blocks. Defenders must get through the screens (we teach our guys to chase off the cutter's tail). The point guard passes to the wing. Defense on the ball must get "ball pressure," and the defenders on the weakside must jump to the pass and be in weakside help. Once the ball is passed to the wing, the player on the strongside block sets a block-to-block screen for the weakside block player, and the passer (point guard) screens away for the weakside wing (Figure 65-A).

Figure 65-A

Figure 65-B

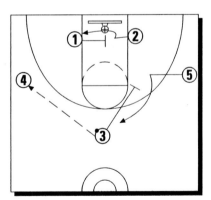

Figure 65-C

- Defense on blocks: The strongside block defender must call "screen," and open up so he can see ball and man and allow the "screened" defender space to get through the screen. Strongside block defender must also check at the lane line before recovering to his man in case his teammate gets screened or has to switch. (We switch on all "like" screens, big-to-big and small-to-small screens.) Weakside defender, who is "head-on-the-rim" on helpside, must check the cutter (his man) and not allow the cutter to rub him off the screen. The weakside defender should force his man to go off the low side of the screen. The defender should always go ballside of the screen.

- Defense on the point guard and weakside wing: The defender on the point guard must call " screen" and stay helpside, allowing his screened teammate to go ballside of the screen. Both defenders must also be aware of the dribble-drive at any time. Offense replaces at the point and also at the weakside wing. Pass from wing to point, the wings downscreen, and the drill begins again (Figure 65-B). Now you have different players occupying different spots, and the defense must deal with small-to-big and big-to-small screens (Figure 65-C).

- Variations: The point guard can pass to the wing and stay at the top of the key rather than screening away for the weakside wing. The wing can pass into the post and then screen for the point. When drill begins, the posts can backscreen for the wings (coach's option).

Coaching Cues:

Offense:

1. Set solid screens, occupy the five spots on the floor.

2. No turnover; be strong with the ball.

3. Ball passed from point to wing = screen away.

4. Ball passed wing to point = downscreen wing to block.

Defense:

1. When the ball is passed, jump to the pass and be ready to help.

2. Communicate on screens.

3. Get ball pressure when your man has the ball.

Coach:

Jerry Dunn is the head basketball coach at Penn State University, where Chris Appleman is an assistant coach.

Drill #66: Help Defense

Purpose:

To improve man-to-man defense off the ball.

Description:

Coach/passer has the ball on the wing (Figure 66-A). There are four defensive players in the lane on help stance. Four offensive players are cutting, trying to receive the ball from the passer. Defenders are focused on not letting offense receive the pass and on helping defend an eventual drive by the passer.

Figure 66-A

Coaching Cues:

1. Defensive stance is low and wide.

2. Stay on pass line.

3. View "your man" and "the ball" at the same time.

4. Be able to close out and/or help on drive to the basket.

5. Be able to block out.

Coach:

Bob Hoffman is the head basketball coach at the University of Texas (Pan American) in Edinburgh, TX. Previously, he coached at Oklahoma Baptist University, where he took the Bison's to six straight consecutive NAIA tournaments and a program of national prominence. Before that, he coached Southern Nazerene University women's team to the NAIA I National Championship in 1989.

Drill #67: Defend the Cutter

Purpose:

To teach defensive players to pressure and contain the ball, to explode to the ball and basket on every pass, and to get over top of screens to defend the cutter going to the basket.

Description:

- Maury John popularized this defensive drill at Drake University. The basic set shown in Figure 67-A is 4-on-4 with the ball at one forward position and a coach or manager at the high post. As the offensive players "V" cut to get open and reverse the ball in Figure 67-B, the weakside guard makes a cut, using the high-post screen.

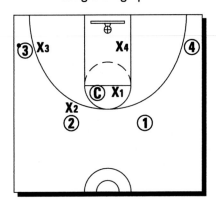

Figure 67-A
4-on-4 Set

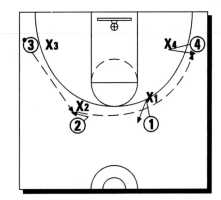

Figure 67-B
Ball is Reversed

Chapter 3—Drills for Defense

- X4 pressures the ball in Figure 67-C, while X2 explodes to the ball to defend the cutter on the ballside (front down the lane) and beat the cutter to the spot in the lane. After the cutter is defended properly, that player (O2) goes back out to the forward position on the same side as the former forward (O3) moves up to the guard position. The ball is now reversed, and the guard cutter is defended on the opposite side. This then becomes a continuous drill.

Coaching Cues:

1. Pressure and contain the ballhandler.

2. Deny the passing lanes.

3. Explode to the ball on each pass.

4. The defender on the cutter must get over the top (Ballside) on the screen and prevent the pass to the cutter.

5. Beat the cutter to the spot.

Coach:

Dick Harter has always been known as a defensive coaching genius. He wrote this article in the Spring '76 *Basketball Bulletin* when he was the head coach at the University of Oregon. Coach Harter presently is an assistant coach for the Indiana Pacers in the NBA.

Figure 67-C
Weakside Cutter

Chapter 3—Drills for Defense

Drill #68: 4-on-3 Contest

Purpose:

To learn to contest every shot.

Description:

Place four offensive players around the arc, passing the ball around (Figure 68-A). Three defenders must guard them. When an offensive player gets an open look, he shoots to score (Figure 68-B).

**Figure 68-A
4-on-3 Set**

**Figure 68-B
Pass and Shoot/Blockout**

Coaching Cues:

1. Contest every shot.

2. Contest off two feet and straight up.

3. Extend one hand high and shout a loud "shot" call.

4. Finish with a block out.

Coach:

Bob Walsh is an assistant basketball coach at Providence College under Tim Welch, who has also had a stint at Iona.

Drill #69: 5-on-4 Defensive Reaction

Purpose:

To teach defensive reaction and recover technique.

Description:

Coach calls "Blue 5-on-4" or "White 5-on-4" to begin a sequence (Figure 69-A). Team must react and take ball from halfcourt. If the coach calls "White 5-on-4", four white team players must quickly adjust and guard five blue people. It is a hustle drill that is designed to develop confidence that a team can stop the other team in out-numbered situations.

Figure 69-A
Blue 5-on-4 Defense

Coaching Cues:

1. Pressure the ballhandler.

2. Prevent penetration.

3. Never run ball to the ballhandler.

Coach:

Tim Cohane is the head basketball coach at the University of Buffalo. He has coached at Dartmouth Merchant Marine Academy and the United States Naval Academy.

Drill #70: Charge and Reaction Drill

Purpose:

To develop quickness and the instinct for reacting to an offensive player who is cutting or dribble driving.

Description:

- Put a player with the ball on both sidelines. The defensive player must react to the first cutter by taking-the-charge (Figure 70-A). When the defensive player jumps back up, he must react to the other line, get a hand up on the shooter, block out, and outlet the ball.

- This drill is a quick reaction exercise. It keeps everyone involved and creates a sense of intensity. The key to the drill is reacting to the penetration using proper technique (Figure 70-B). This drill covers helpside defense, individual close outs, rebounding, and charge technique for quickness. As a rule, this drill is very intense. If the defensive player does not capture the rebound, he must go until he stops the play (Figure 70-C).

Figure 70-A
Take Charge

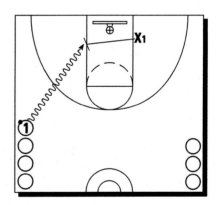

Figure 70-B
Stop Penetration

Coaching Cues:

1. The defensive player must be quick and react.

2. Sell the charge using proper technique, recovery and reaction to the next driver.

3. Contest every shot and capture the ball after blocking-out (hot feet, find shooter, tag, and get the ball).

Coach:

Tony Dominguez is the assistant basketball coach at Western Washington University. He has assisted Brad Jackson for two years in their successful NAIA/NCAA II program.

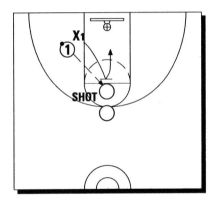

Figure 70-C
Contest Shot-Blockout

Drill #71: 3-on-3 Fullcourt Drill

Purpose:

To teach players to pressure and contain the ballhandler, to deny the guard-to-forward pass, and to provide help to defense.

Description:

• In Figure 71-A, three offensive players inbound the ball and bring it up the floor. The inbounder cannot throw ball beyond free-throw line extended. When ball is inbounds, defenders pressure the ball and play good-position defense away from the ball.

- With the ball in the front court, the offensive players are spaced 15-18 ft. apart on the wings. The middle player can either pass and cut or pass and screen away, as seen in Figure 71-B. No shots are allowed.

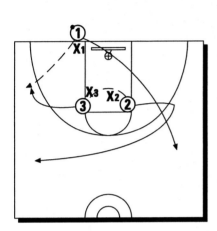

Figure 71-A
3-on-3 Front Court

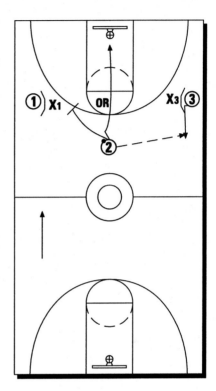

Figure 71-B
3-on-3 Ball
Out-of-Bounds

Coaching Cues:

1. Pressure and contain ball.

2. Deny the lead pass ahead.

3. Help with vision.

4. Coach may also allow passes only (no dribbling).

Coach:

Nolan Richardson has coached at both the community college level and the four-year college level, where he was won national championships. His Arkansas Razorback teams are noted for their pressure defense and uptempo style of play.

Drill #72: Box and Board from the Zone Defense

Purpose:

To teach players to effectively rebound in a zone defense situation.

Description:

- Coaches can select any zone position or situation where a shot can be taken. When the coach or offensive player shoots, all five defenders must carry out their box-out assignment or box out an offensive player from their zone coverage area (Figure 72-A).

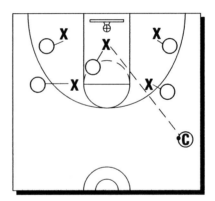

Figure 72-A

- As seen in Figure 72-B, defenders attempt to create a defensive box-out area "in the paint." The coach may keep defensive team in position for a number of successful box outs and may also make his defenders transition to offense.

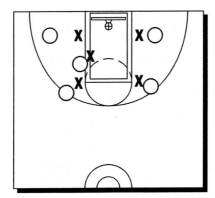

Figure 72-B

Coaching Cues:

1. The defensive players must be in a defensive recovering position.

2. Players must box out to the point where they create a box in the key (paint).

3. The primary objective of the drill is to box out where the ball hits the court surrounded by defensive players.

Coach:

John Banks is an assistant coach under head coach Joe Expisito at Angelo State University (TX), where the Runnin' Rams have had their most wins in the last four years.

4

COMBINATION DRILLS

Drill #73: Practice Sessions–Drills and Fundamentals

Purpose:

To improve the ability of players to perform offensive and defensive fundamental skills (1-on-1, 2-on-2).

Description

- Normally, we break our workouts down into two categories: PRESEASON and IN-SEASON. We do not work more than two days in a row. An example of our schedule would be: work Monday and Tuesday, and give Wednesday off; work Thursday and Friday, and give Saturday and Sunday off.

- If our practice goes two hours, we have a pretty good team. If our practice lasts as long as three hours, we have some shortcomings. The NCAA says that we may start on October 15. When I speak of preseason, I am talking about that period of time between October 15 and December 1.

- Before the season starts, several questions must be answered. What we want to cover during the preseason must be decided. The categories which need to be taught must be organized. After you know what needs to be covered, then those things should be broken into two- and three-man drills.

- Normally, we operate between offense and defense. We like to go sixty percent offense and forty percent defense. Most of our drills are used to work on both offense and defense. We do like to alternate our drills from offense to defense and vice versa.

- Each of the drills will usually last from ten to twenty minutes, depending on the execution of the drill. The first hour and a half is spent on two- and three-man drills. The second part of the workout is usually five-on-five. We usually go halfcourt first, then fullcourt. We scrimmage about two times a week with officials.

- During the season, we take the day off after a game unless we have a game the following night. The length of the workouts before a game are one hour to an hour and a half. The first part of practice is drills. The second part of the workout is used to go over the opponent's offense and defense, and then the offense and defense we are to use. From our scouting report, we go over characteristics of individuals of the opposing team.

- What are some of the drills we use? Some of these drills I have used for twenty years. You might use imagination and come up with your own. All of our drills involve fundamentals and are part of our offense and defense.

- We start out with one-on-one drills. We break the group into three lines and work on offense and defense simultaneously (Figure 73-A). 1 passes to 2 and goes behind to get the ball. 2 gives the ball to 3 and assumes the position of a weakside defensive man. 3 passes the ball back to 1 and goes to play one-on-one defense.

Figure 73-A

- This action creates a one-on-one on the side. This is a good drill because it creates several situations: 1) teach defenders to force the drive to the middle for help; 2) force him laterally; 3) makes it difficult to make a move; 4) if 1 beats 3, then 2 helps and 3 chases; 5) if the shot is taken, we stress blocking off. This is the first drill we teach. If the shot is missed, the guy with the ball plays offense, the other two men defend him.

- We also work one-on-one from the middle (Figure 73-B). In this drill 1 passes to 2 and goes outside and takes up a help position. 2 passes to 3 and goes to get the ball back. 3 then guards 2 on the one-on-one. 1 is the helper. The same ideas are presented. They must block out on the shot.

Figure 73-B

- The next thing we teach is defensing the screen. We use the same set up (see Figures 73-C and 73-D). We believe in mixing the guys up. We have a big guy play a little guy and a little guy play a big guy. This drill begins by 1 passing to 2 and cutting inside to set a screen on the lane. 2 passes to 3 and goes to get the ball back.

- 3 defenses 2 again, but this time, he is learning how to fight the screen. 3 slides over 1 and then does it again when 2 reverses his dribble. A number of things are taught in this drill, including getting over the top of a screen; getting in between the screen and defensive teammate; getting the roll man to switch in order to prevent the pick-and-roll; and the hedge.

- In this drill, you want to teach 3 what to do. The first time, 2 should go over the top and tell 2 to do it off of the dribble. 3, as 2 starts, should try to go

Chapter 4—Combination Drills

over the top. If he makes it, come back over the top again (Figure 73-D). 3 must be in tight. He does it twice, and then 2 takes the shot. If free the first time over, 3 should then take the shot.

- We like to do this drill from the same position only now we add another man and create two-on-two situation (Figure 73-E). By adding another man you can teach the switch can be taught from this drill, and a voice call can be used on the screen. The new man yells "pick right or left."

Figure 73-C

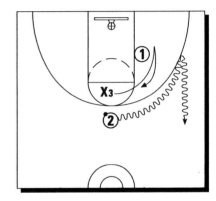

Figure 73-D

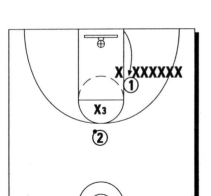

Figure 73-E

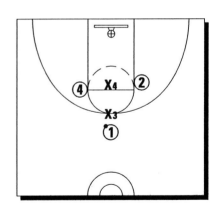

Figure 73-F

- In teaching the pick and roll, a helpside man, X4, can be incorporated into the drill in order to have weakside help on the pick and roll (see Figure 73-F). This is an excellent exercise to teach technique in the pick and roll. 2 and 4 are the screeners. 1 can dribble off either side to create the pick and roll on either side. 3 defenses it by playing 1.

- From this same set, we can teach how to "beat the man to the spot" (Figure 73-G). 1 passes to 2 and goes outside. 2 passes to 3 and takes up the weakside-help position. 3 passes to 1 and goes to defense him one-on-one. Figure 73-H shows 1 with the ball and 3 on defense against him. The new offensive player, 4, tries to come to the ball. 2 impedes his progress to the middle of the lane. This drill creates the two-on-two again. 2 must beat 4 to the ball. There are several things you can teach from this drill, including to play one-on-one; to force to help; to adjust to passes and help; to see the ball and the assigned man; to point to the ball.

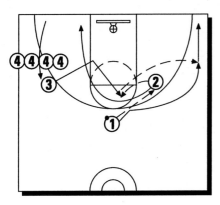

Figure 73-G   **Figure 73-H**

- We have a drill to teach overplay. The overplay is taught to prevent a scoring threat. The coach should be sure to teach the defense the backdoor move. The drill should be like a game as much as possible. The drill we use is off of the pass-and-go-away move (Figure 73-1). 1 passes to 2 and goes away to screen for 3; 3 cuts across to the ball and defenses 2. 1 spins outside and comes back to his original spot.

- We tell 3 not to play for the steal, but just force him high and wide. 2 may return pass to 1 and make a backdoor cut to the basket. If he wants to go backdoor, the defender should use his elbow to slow his cut. On the backdoor cut, we open to the ball.

- We have designed drills to practice all types of defensive techniques. We can also teach defensing the pivot. We constrict the area to teach defensing the post (Figure 73-J). We set up the post man inside pass the ball outside, and have the defense slide with the ball. When the ball moves, we want our defensive man to go over the top and set up on the baseline side. We tell our defensive man not to make contact. We don't want to tell the offense where he is located. We do this every day until deep into the season.

- I like these drills very much because we can work on offensive and defensive things at the same time.

Coaching Cues:

See article above. Coaches should expose players to as many game situations as possible. Drills should be structured that are a regular part of your offense and defense, whenever possible.

Coach:

Lou Carnesecca and his famous colored sweater wardrobe became landmarks at St. John's University (NY) where, in 24 years of coaching, he led his teams to postseason play every year (18 NCAAS, 6 NITS). He was national Coach of the Year in 1983 and 1985, and was inducted into the Basketball Hall of Fame in 1992.

Drill #74: Black and Gold Rebounding

Purpose:

To teach players basic techniques of offensive and defensive rebounding in a team competition.

Description:

The black-gold team rebounding is shown in Figures 74-A and 74-B. The first phase is shown in Figure 74-A.

- #1 and #2 versus A and B. #1 throws a pass to A who shoots. If this first shot goes in, it should be played as a missed shot out of the net. #1 and #2 box out A and B, as all four fight for the rebound. If #1 and #2 get the ball, they shoot right away or play 2 on 2 versus A and B. If A and B get the rebound, they then attempt to score.

- Teams that score go to the end of lines under the basket. Teams that do not score go to end of line out front. At end of a certain amount of time, the losing team runs.

- We can further concentrate on rebounding in any other drill that is used by assigning a point total for each offensive and defensive rebound. This is usually done in a five-on-five halfcourt situation.

- **5-on-5 Rebounding Drill** (Figure 74-B). We concentrate on rebounding with a 5-on-5 drill. The offense runs normal offense. When the shot goes up, all players go for the rebound. Points of +1 for offensive rebounds, +2 for defensive rebounds, or any other point total may be used depending on what part of rebounding you want to emphasize. Give a certain amount of possessions.

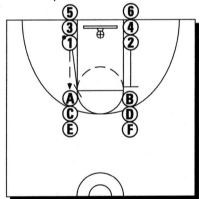

Figure 74-A

Figure 74-B

- Immediate reinforcement must follow all competition. There must be immediate rewards and punishments riding on the outcome of each competitive activity. We have players set the punishments before the competitive drill takes place. This self-imposed punishment results in stronger self discipline and helps to maintain a better coach-player relationship.

Coaching Cues:

1. Thoroughly teach each drill and how it fits your style of play.

2. Make the drill competitive.

3. Let the players determine the consequences of winning and losing the drill.

Coach:

Don Showalter wrote this article for the Summer '86 *Basketball Bulletin* while coaching at Mid-Prairie High School in Colorado.

Drill #75: Rebound Game

Purpose:

To teach the principles of rebounding positioning and block-out techniques.

Description:

- The "rebound game" is a 5-on-5 halfcourt competition with great possibilities for teaching the importance of rebounding. Scoring is simple. Teams are awarded one point for a defensive rebound, one point for being fouled, and two points for an offensive rebound. After determining which team receives the ball first, teams alternate possessions. The offense keeps possession until either it scores or the defense gets a rebound or forces a turnover. On all changes of possession, the ball must be checked by the coach who stands on the sideline at about the top of the key extended (Figure 75-A).

Figure 75-A

- The game can be played either to a predetermined score (i.e., first team to 20), or for a specified number of minutes with time displayed on the scoreboard clock. This is a very competitive drill.

Coaching Cues:

1. Be alert on change of possession.

2. Adjust quickly from offense to defense.

Coach:

Dave Frohman has coached basketball for more than twenty-five years at the high school and college levels. He is currently the head basketball coach at Dickinson College. He has coached the Red Devils to four post season playoffs in the NCAA III National Tournament.

Drill #76: 4-on-4 Transition Drill

Purpose:

To teach the quick change from offensive to defense and defense to offense.

Description:

- Start with four defensive players spread along the foul line, one at each corner of the foul line and one on each wing. Have four offensive players line up along the baseline opposite the four defenders. The drill begins when you throw the ball to one of the offensive players and call the name of a defensive player. The player whose name you call must run, touch the baseline, and then sprint to help the other three defenders who are retreating and defending the opposite basket.

- The offensive players run the primary and secondary break (if necessary), while the defensive players communicate and help each other until the fourth defensive player recovers. (The offense is typically forced into the secondary break because the defense should have enough players back by then to shut down the primary break.)

- This drill can be done with any number of players, from 2-on-2 through 5-on-5.

The drill ends when the offensive team scores or turns the ball over, or the defense rebounds a miss. See Figure 76-A.

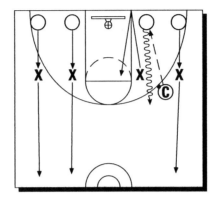

Figure 76-A
4-on-4 Transition

Coaching Cues:

1. The defense should stop the ball at free-throw line level.

2. The lay-up should not be given up.

3. The wings stay wide on the break.

4. The defense sprints with vision to stop the ball.

Coach:

Morgan Wootten is the basketball coach at DeMatha High School in Washington, D.C. Many regard him as one of the best high school coaches in the history of the game.

Drill #77: Advantage Transition Drill

Purpose:

To teach players to pass, catch, and shoot in transition, while improving their decision-making skills.

Description:

• A full-court drill that progressively builds from a 1-on-1 situation to a 2-on-2, to 3-on-2, etc., and finishes 5-on-5 (Figure 77-A and 77-B). Two teams consisting of five players each match-up with each pair assuming a number 1 through 5. Each team lines up in order on opposite baselines. Team A, Player 1 begins with the ball on offense. Team B, Player 1 plays defense in a fullcourt, 1-on-1 situation. Since Team A began with the ball, Team B will have all the advantage situations in transition. The drill progresses as such: 1-on-1, 2-on-1, 3-on-2, 3-on-3, 4-on-3, 4-on-4, 5-on-4, and finally 5-on-5. After each shot or loss of possession, the opposing team either inbounds the ball (on a make) or immediately transitions the other way with the appropriate player entering the drill to make it either an even situation or an advantage situation.

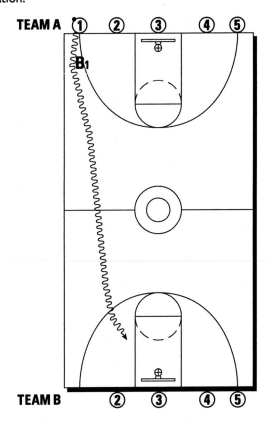

Figure 77-A

Chapter 4—Combination Drills

- Once all five players from both teams have participated, the drill stops. The opposite team restarts the drill (Team B in this case), and all advantage situations will be in Team A's favor. The drill should start with the opposite number (5) the second time through to ensure equal participation time for all players.

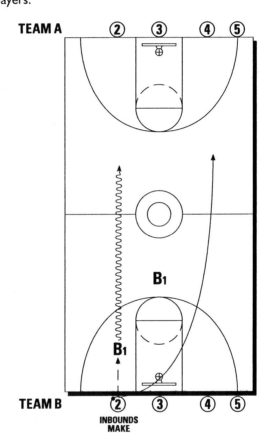

Figure 77-B

Coaching Cues:

1. The ball must be inbounded after each score,

2. The players should look to push the ball in transition.

3. Players waiting on the baseline must be alert and ready to transition.

Coach:

Heather Kirk is an assistant women's basketball coach at Fordham University, after a stint in the Army.

Drill #78: Team Challenge

Purpose:

To set values for what the coach wants to emphasize.

Description:

- Start the drill in your secondary set. If the offense scores, they get the ball back at halfcourt. On a turn over or if the defense gets a steal or a rebound, the game is in transition, and the other team's fast-break basket would be worth two points. If they score or not, they still get a halfcourt possession.

- **Scoring:** One point, ball reversal; one point, post entry; one point, made basket; one point, get fouled; two points, offensive rebound; the opponents score goes to 0 if the defense draws a charge; and two points for a transition basket. Game is to 15 points.

Coaching Cues:

Select a point of emphasis each time you run the drill.

Coach:

Craig Jacobson is the new head basketball coach at Doane College, in Nebraska, after twenty years in the high-school ranks. He replaces the legendary Bob Erickson.

Drill #79: Full Court, Five-on-Five, Double Whistle Drill

Purpose:

To teach the players to respond quickly to a double whistle so that the coach can point out correct or incorrect behavior.

Description:

- Whenever the coach sees any obvious mistake on the court from which all players in a full court, five-on-five situation can profit, he double whistles. At that signal, all players must instantly freeze in position so that the coach can point out and correct the mistake for the benefit of all. We use this drill frequently with excellent results. The diagrammed play is an example of a situation calling for a double whistle.

- Offensive players are O1, O2, O3, O4, and O5; defensive players are X1, X2, X3, X4, and X5. O1 passes up court to O3, who dribbles, stops, and shoots, with X3 in good defensive position. O4 is in the left corner. Once O3 started to dribble, we would double whistle. As soon as he received the ball, he should have passed to O4. If O4 had received the pass and dribbled toward the basket, either he or O5, coming in from the other side, would get a lay-up. See Figure 79-A.

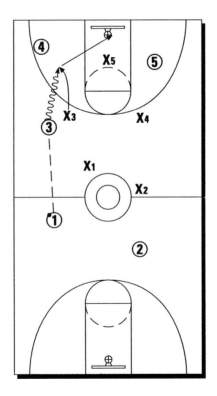

Figure 79-A

Coaching Cues:

Coaches can stop any situation to emphasize a coaching cue for the whole team. Assistants can still focus on individual cues while coaching "on the run."

Coach:

Bob Cousy, a Boston Celtic great, is a member of the Basketball Hall of Fame and current announcer for the Boston Celtics. Cousy coached at Boston College and the Kansas City Kings of the NBA. Some consider him one of the best point-guard ballhandlers in the history of professional basketball.

Drill #80: Hedge Drill

Purpose:

To teach the fundamentals of "pick and roll" offense and defense.

Description:

- This is a three-on-three drill that works on the pick-and-roll offense and defense plus weakside defense. The offensive player with the ball looks at turning the corner to attack the basket. Many areas of fundamental basketball are covered.

- Offensively, the drill reviews ballhandling, spacing, and footwork on screens. Defensively, the drill reviews footwork, moving through the screen, defending the screen, weakside help, and blocking out.

Coaching Cues:

Dribble by the screen shoulder to shoulder with the screener. The screener utilizes a wide base and rolls toward the basket, always facing ball and showing his target hand, or he steps out for outside shot (Figure 80-A). The defender on the screener hedges out to force the ballhandler wide. On the hedge he should maintain contact with screener. The weakside defender should cross the middle of the rim to give help on the roll. Defending the ball, he should force the ballhandler to go over the top of the pick and force him higher and wider, while defender goes over the top of screen. Continuous play for a "repick" as seen in Figure 80-B.

| Figure 80-A | Figure 80-B |

Coach:

Eric Musselman is an assistant basketball coach for the Orlando Magic under Chuck Daly. Hall of Famer Chuck Daly directed the Detroit Pistons to back-to-back NBA Championships in 1989 and 1990, and guided the original U.S. Olympic Dream Team to a gold medal in 1992. Chuck has coached at the high school, college and professional levels.

Drill #81: Trap Drill

Purpose:

To teach players how to handle defensive pressure and double-team situations and to teach defenders to set proper "traps."

Description:

- The drill uses three offensive and three defensive players (Figure 81-A).

- The two defensive players should trap the ball, and the other defensive player splits the difference of the two remaining offensive players, as seen in Figure 81-B.

- First, the offensive player with the ball is not allowed to dribble. Later he is permitted one dribble after the defensive players have acquired the capability to effectively trap the offensive player and split the difference of the two offensive players (Figure 81-C).

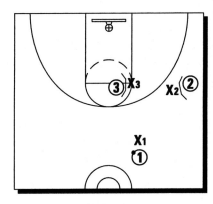

Figure 81-A

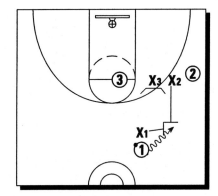

Figure 81-B

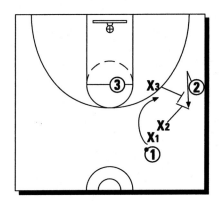

Figure 81-C

Coaching Cues:

1. Offense: Firm up—be strong with the ball; step through the trap; don't turn your back to other offensive players; fake a pass to make a pass; step to meet the pass; and catch the pass with two hands.

2. Defense: Set active, legal traps; maintain active feet, keep a knee-to-knee position by the trappers; keep hands up; and trace the ball.

Coach:

Phil Pearson is the assistant basketball coach at the University of Alabama under head coach Mark Gottfried.

Drill #82: Circle Trap

Purpose:

To build ball-strong and dynamic moves; to eliminate turnovers; and to teach defensive players to trap the ball without fouling.

Description:

- Offensive players must keep one foot at all times on the center circle (Figure 82-A). When the offense receives the ball, they should sweep the floor and creat space. The offense should always fake a pass to make a pass. The offense should remain ball strong and dynamic. The defensive players should attack with hard traps. The defense should step through the trap if necessary. Later in the season, one back dribble can be added to the drill.

- Drill is over when the defense gets a deflection or causes a turnover (Figure 82-B). If drill goes too long without one of the above, the coach ends the drill.

Coaching Cues:

1. The defenders use the fundamental trapping techniques — active feet, knee-to-knee position, and hands up tracing the ball.

2. Offensive players be strong with the ball, clear space, face the defense, and see the whole floor.

Coach:

Matthew Driscoll is the assistant basketball coach at Clemson University under Larry Shyatt. Larry Shyatt returns to Clemson as head coach where he was an assistant.

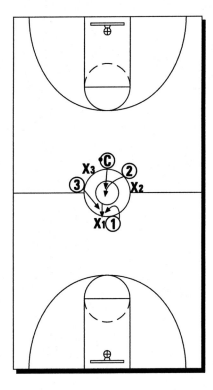

Figure 82-A

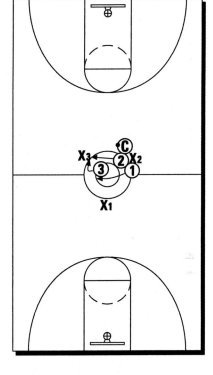

Figure 82-B

Chapter 4—Combination Drills

ABOUT THE EDITORS

Jerry Krause has coached and taught basketball at all levels (elementary, secondary, college and Olympic) for over thirty years. Krause has written twelve basketball books and produced eighteen videos on the sport. He has been research chair for the National Association of Basketball Coaches (NABC) since 1968, and is on the Board of Directors. He has served the longest tenure (15 years) of anyone on the NCAA Basketball Rules Committee, where he was chairman; he also served as President of the NAIA Basketball Coaches Association.

Dr. Krause received the 1998 NABC Cliff Wells Appreciation Award for lifetime contributions to the game. He presently serves as professor of sport philosophy and director of instruction in the Department of Physical Education at the United States Military Academy, West Point, New York.

Jim Conn is an experienced coaching educator who has coached successfully at the high school and college levels. He presently teaches at Central Missouri State University.

CONTRIBUTOR INDEX